AF600408

THE COLLEGIATE TRIBUNAL OF FIRST INSTANCE

THE CATHOLIC UNIVERSITY OF AMERICA
CANON LAW STUDIES
Number 78

THE COLLEGIATE TRIBUNAL OF FIRST INSTANCE

WITH SPECIAL REFERENCE TO MATRIMONIAL CAUSES

A DISSERTATION

Submitted to the Faculty of the School of Canon Law of the Catholic University of America in Partial Fulfillment of the Requirements for the Degree of Doctor of Canon Law

BY

AVITUS EDWARD LYONS, S.T.B., J.C.L.,
Priest of the Diocese of Toledo

THE CATHOLIC UNIVERSITY OF AMERICA
WASHINGTON, D. C.
1932

Nihil Obstat:
LUDOVICUS H. MOTRY, S.T.D., J.C.D.,
Censor Deputatus.
Washingtonii, D. C., die xii Maii, 1932.

Imprimatur:
CAROLUS J. ALTER, D.D.,
Ep. Toletanus.
Toleti, die xviii Maii, 1932.

Printed by
THE PAULIST PRESS
New York, N. Y.

TO MARY IMMACULATE

MOTHER OF GOD

TABLE OF CONTENTS

PART III

PROCEDURE IN MATRIMONIAL CAUSES PROPER TO THE DIOCESAN COLLEGIATE TRIBUNAL OF FIRST INSTANCE

ABBREVIATIONS

AAS—Acta Apostolicae Sedis.
AER—The American Ecclesiastical Review.
AkKR—Archiv fur katholisches Kirchenrecht.
Apoll.—Apollinaris.
ASS—Acta Sanctae Sedis.
C.—Canon seu caput (iuris antiqui).
Cc.—Canones seu capita (iuris antiqui).
Can.—Canon (novi Codicis).
Cans.—Canones (novi Codicis).
Coll.—Collectanea Sacra Congregationis de Propaganda Fide.
Coll. Lac.—(Collectio Lacensis) Acta et Decreta Sacrorum Conciliorum Recentiorum.
D.—Digesta vel Distinctio.
Fontes—Codicis Iuris Canonici Fontes.
Jus Pont.—Jus Pontificium.
Mansi—Sacrorum Conciliorum Nova et Amplissima Collectio.
MPG—(Migne, Patrologia Graeca) Migne, Jacques Paul, Patrologiae Cursus Completus—Series Graeca.
MPL—(Migne, Patrologia Latina) Migne, Jacques Paul, Patrologiae Cursus Completus—Series Latina.
NRT—Nouvelle Revue Theologique.
Periodica—Periodica de Re Canonica et Morali Utili praesertim Religiosis et Missionariis.
Pont. Com. Int. Cod.—Pontificia Commissio ad Codicis Canones Authentice Interpretandos.
S. C. C.—Sacra Congregatio Concilii.
S. C. de Sac.—Sacra Congregatio de Sacramentis.
S. C. EE. et RR.—Sacra Congregatio Episcoporum et Regularium.
S. C. S. Off.—Sacra Congregatio Sancti Officii.
S. R. R.—Sacra Romana Rota.

FOREWORD

The subject of this dissertation, THE COLLEGIATE TRIBUNAL OF FIRST INSTANCE, With Special Reference to Matrimonial Causes, is treated in the fourth book of the Code in Canons 1572, 1576, 1577, 1578, 1614, 1615 and 1871.

No attempt is made in these pages to establish or prove the judiciary power of the Church. This is presupposed as an established fact.

Part One of this dissertation contains a brief historical introduction to the subject. From the limited sources of historical material at hand it has been possible to give only a brief resume of the course of development of the collegiate tribunal throughout the ages. A short sketch of the history of formal procedure in matrimonial causes of nullity is added.

Part Two of this dissertation considers the constitution of the tribunal, the various duties of the members of the tribunal and the general principles regulating the proceedings of the tribunal.

In Part Three a general outline of a trial in matrimonial causes proper to the tribunal is given.

It has not been considered necessary to include within the scope of this dissertation copies of judicial formulas or documents, since these may easily be found in such standard works as *Bouix, Lega, Monacelli, Pierantonelli, D'Angelo, Cocchi,* and in the various issues of the *Acta Apostolicae Sedis.*

The writer takes this occasion to express his sincere gratitude to the Most Reverend Karl J. Alter, D.D., present Bishop of Toledo, and to the Most Reverend Samuel A. Stritch, D.D., former Bishop of Toledo, for the opportunity of advanced studies and for their kindly interest. He wishes also to express his gratitude to the members of the Faculty of Canon Law for their timely and helpful assistance in the preparation of this study.

INTRODUCTION

A COLLEGIATE tribunal of judges may be defined as a group or board of judges who act collectively and simultaneously hear and decide cases by a majority vote.

The collegiate tribunal as a court of original jurisdiction seems to be of Germanic rather than of Roman origin. The judge sole system prevailed in Roman Procedure, although the custom and sometimes the duty of a judge sole assuming *assessores* who had only a consultative vote [1] is very plainly stated in the sources.[2]

Novel 23, 2 seems to point to the existence of the collegiate tribunal where the law declares that if a cause is heard in first instance by several judges it should on appeal be heard by a college of judges numerically equal to the number of judges of the court of first instance. The Code [3] speaks of courts of appeal composed of several judges.

There are many reasons to discourage a positive statement on the question, yet this principle of collegial courts seems to have developed out of the consolidation of the judge president and judgment-finders of the early Germanic courts.[4] In keeping with tradition, German juridical inclination has been for the collegial courts, and all the more important and presumably more difficult causes have been dealt with by courts of this character. From Germany this idea spread throughout the judicial systems of other continental nations notably France, Austria, Spain and Italy. The institution has been continued even in the modern reforms of European judiciary law. For example, in Germany the Reform of 1924 retained the *Oberlandesgericht* and the *Reichgericht,* courts which require the necessary participation of several judges in making decisions. In ancient French law one finds the *enquête* and the institution of collegial

[1] Pertile, *Storia della procedura,* 2. ed., I, 215 sq.

[2] *Digest.* I, 22; IX, 3; IV, 2.

[3] *Code* VII, 62, 32, 4; Code VII, 62, 34.

[4] Cfr. Engelmann-Millar, *History of Continental Civil Procedure,* VII, 546, n. 14.

courts are still in existence in the courts of *Cassation* and of *Arrondissement*. In Italy courts of appeal and courts of cassation are collegial bodies.[5]

In the United States system of courts, collegial courts are primarily courts of appeal with the Supreme Court of the United States at the top of the legal structure. This court is presided over by nine justices, a Chief Justice and eight Associate Justices. While this court is primarily a court of appeal, the Constitution declares that it shall have original jurisdiction in all cases affecting ambassadors and other public ministers and consuls and those in which a state is party.[6] Besides the Supreme Court of the United States each state has likewise a supreme court composed of several judges which acts as a court of appeal.

The collegiate tribunal in Canon Law is modern only in the sense that the present legislation demands that it be set up in every diocese throughout the world as an ordinary stable tribunal of the diocesan court of first instance. Formerly with the exception of Roman tribunals and certain other tribunals established by particular legislation collegiate tribunals functioned more frequently as delegated tribunals of the Holy See than as tribunals of original jurisdiction.

The collegiate tribunal of the diocesan court of first instance is today composed of three or five judges according to the requirements of the Sacred Canons in which its services are demanded or permitted. The Ordinary or the Official or the Vice-Official usually presides with two or four synodal or pro-synodal judges as associate judges.

The tribunal has competency in both contentious and criminal causes according to the prescriptions of the Sacred Canons. Contentious causes are those in which the subject matter of a trial concerns the prosecution or the vindication of the rights of physical or moral persons, or the declaration of juridical facts concerning such persons. Criminal causes are causes in which the infliction or declaration of a penalty for a crime is the object of the trial.

The organization and personnel of the collegiate tribunal of an

[5] Engelmann-Millar, *o.c.*, p. 805.

[6] Willoughby, *Principles of Judicial Administration*, p. 240.

archdiocese when it exercises judicial power proper to the court of first instance of an archbishop's diocese is identical in form and construction to the tribunal of any other diocese.

PART I

HISTORICAL INTRODUCTION

CHAPTER I

THE HISTORICAL DEVELOPMENT OF THE COLLEGIATE TRIBUNAL

HISTORICALLY the collegiate tribunal as an institution of Canon Law may be surveyed under a threefold division:

1. From the first to the twelfth century.
2. The Decretal Age.
3. Particular legislation of the nineteenth century.

ART. I. COLLEGIATE TRIBUNALS FROM THE FIRST TO THE TWELFTH CENTURY

Documentary evidence of ecclesiastical court procedure in the first few centuries of the Church's existence is scarce. The bishop was the recognized judge in ecclesiastical affairs in each community.[1] The process itself was simple and informal in which the substance of justice and court procedure was observed.[2] The bishop *praesentibus senioribus* surrounded by his priests heard the charge or accusation viva voce proposed, listened to the witnesses and the defense, and immediately passed sentence.[3]

Towards the middle of the fourth century there is evidence of tribunals of several judges in the canons of the first three Councils of Carthage. These councils decreed that when any charge was brought against a bishop, a priest or a deacon, a court of twelve bishops was necessary to hear a charge against a bishop, five bishops for the trial of a priest, and two bishops for the trial of a deacon.[4] The Council of Constantinople (394) declared that henceforth a bishop was not to be tried by three judges much less by two, but by

[1] *Didascalia,* II, 22, 23—Funk, *Didascalia et Constitutiones Apostolorum* I, pp. 84-114.

[2] Hurter—*Compendium Theologiae Dogmaticae* III, p. 551.

[3] C. 23, D. LXXXVI; c. 2, CXV, q. 7.

[4] I. C. of Carthage (348), c. 3—Mansi, III, 685; II C. of Carthage (390), c. 4,—Mansi, III, 691; III C. of Carthage (397), c. 5—Mansi, III, 867.

a synod of Bishops or by a provincial council.[5] The third canon of the Council of Sardica concerned judicial controversies. It ordained that when a bishop unsuccessful in a court of first instance appealed to Rome, the Pope would constitute a tribunal of neighboring bishops to try the case on appeal.[6] Canon five of the same council speaks of a tribunal of bishops.

Pope Gelasius (492-496) sent Stephan, Herculentius and Justus to Spain as a tribunal of delegated judges to review the cases of Antiochus, a priest, and Leonicus.[7] The *Constitutiones Apostolorum*, probably a fifth century collection, speaks of the bishop presiding in court assisted by his priests and deacons having only a consultative vote.[8] Gratian quotes the African Councils held at this time as requiring a council of bishops to condemn a bishop.[9] The Council of Tribur (895) decreed that a bishop could be tried only by a court of twelve bishops, a priest by six bishops, and a deacon by three bishops.[10]

Art. II. Collegiate Tribunals in the Decretal Age

When Gratian in the second part of his work treats of judges, he seems to speak of them as single judges rather than as members of a collegiate tribunal. Nevertheless in Causa VI, quaestio 4, he quotes the canons of the ancient councils which require a court of several judges to try cases against bishops, priests and deacons. It may be presumed that he is giving the practice of his day when he demands that a college of six bishops try a priest, and three bishops try a deacon. Clergy of lower rank than a deacon were to be tried in the presence of the bishop and clergy in the diocesan synod. A bishop could be judged only by a college of twelve bishops.[11]

The Decretals of Gregory, the Liber Sextus, the Clementinae, and the Extravagantes give us the practice of the thirteenth and

[5] Mansi, III, 851.

[6] Hefele-Clarke, *A History of Christian Councils*, II, 112.

[7] C. 10, D. LIV.

[8] Funk, *Didascalia et Constitutiones Apostolorum*, I, 576.

[9] Cc. 1-7, C. XV, q. 7.

[10] Mansi, VIII, 329.

[11] Cc. 1. 2, C. III, q. 8.

the succeeding centuries. The first, second and fifth books of Gregory IX are the most important for this study. The Liber Sextus, the Clementinae and the Extravagantes give us very little new matter.

Pope Coelestine III [12] declared that it had been the custom of the Holy See to delegate more than one judge for the settlement of a case, because a sentence given by a college of judges seemed to give more security for a correct sentence. During this age it seems to have been the practice of the Holy See to delegate a college of judges, rather than a single judge to hear causes that were reserved to it by law, or by special reservation, or that were taken to Rome initially or appealed to Rome.

These delegated tribunals were appointed either *in solidum* or *simpliciter*. If they were appointed *in solidum* that is, if their mandate read *"ut omnes, aut duo, vel unus mandatum exequantur, aut exequatur,"* or if similar terms were used the cause might be heard and decided either by all of the delegated judges or by two or even by one of them. If one of them had begun to hear or try the cause without the others, the latter could not interfere or take part in the proceedings, save in case the delegated judge who began to hear the cause was hindered or maliciously refused to go ahead.[13]

If they were appointed not *in solidum* but *simpliciter*, without the above quoted clause or any similar clause empowering them to act or proceed separately; in other words if the instrument or mandate of their appointment simply stated that a certain cause or class of causes was committed to them, and did not state that they could proceed individually or separately, then they must proceed collectively or in a body, and one could not hear the cause without the others, even where one of them was legitimately hindered or had died. Otherwise the proceedings were *ipso jure* null and void, unless the letter of appointment stated differently.[14] If several were appointed to hear the same cause in these or similar words: *"Ut si omnes interesse nequiverint, reliqui mandatum exequantur,"* they had to proceed collectively or in a body; but if one or the other of

[12] C. 21, X, *de officio et potestate judicis delegati,* I, 29.

[13] C. 8, *de officio et potestate judicis delegati,* I. 14, in VI°.

[14] C. 16, X, *de officio judicis delegati,* I. 29.

them was absent by reason of a legitimate excuse, the rest could proceed without the absentee provided his excuse was properly communicated to the remaining delegated judges. Without such notification of absence, the other judges could not proceed and if they, nevertheless, did proceed their acts were null and void. In the event that one of the judges refused to act or attend when he was not lawfully hindered, the rest could proceed as soon as they had certain or undoubted information of the refusal on the part of their colleague.[15]

In all cases where a matter was to be adjudicated by several persons collectively, the opinion of the majority was to be followed and the majority decided the sentence. When the votes were equally divided, recourse was to be taken to the superior from whom the delegation emanated.[16] If one of the delegated judges was suspected, all were disqualified until the suspicion was removed.[17] Exceptions against the delegated judges might be taken against one of the associate judges or against the tribunal as a whole. In a college of two judges or more, the unchallenged judges decided the case of their colleague.[18] If the entire college was challenged the delegating authority would decide whether the objection was to be sustained.[19]

The power of these delegated collegiate tribunals was measured by the superior delegating, and the kind and number of causes committed to them was expressly stated in the mandate or commission appointing them. If they went beyond their mandate their acts were null and void.[20] They could however decide those matters or questions which, though not directly committed to them, were nevertheless conneced with or accessory to the matter of the causes delegated to them.[21]

Various pieces of legislation came from Rome at different times

[15] C. 21, X, *de officio judicis delegati,* I. 29; Schmalzgrueber, *Jus Ecclesiasticum Universum,* Lib. I, Tit. XXIX, n. 17.

[16] Bouix, *De Judiciis Ecclesiasticis,* I, 151.

[17] Barbosa, *Jus Pontificium Universum,* I, 254.

[18] C. 4, *de officio et potestate judicis delegati,* I. 14, in VI°.

[19] Cc. 36, 41, 61, X, *de appellationibus recusationibus et relationibus,* II, 28: c. 4, X, *de foro competenti,* II, 2.

[20] Cc. 32, 37, X, *de officio et potestate judicis delegati,* I, 29.

[21] C. 5, X, *de officio et potestate judicis delegati,* I, 29.

during this period, relative to the quality of these judges, who were to enjoy papal jurisdiction. Because of the great distances of the various sees from Rome, and the difficulties of communication in that period, it frequently happened that the Pope knew little or nothing concerning the quality of persons enjoying this jurisdiction. In order that the Holy See might be represented by worthy persons Boniface VIII, in his constitution *Statutum,* decreed that no person could fulfill this office of delegated judge unless he were a canon of a cathedral church or endowed with an ecclesiastical dignity or possessed of a personate. The hearing of cases by virtue of Papal delegation was to take place only in great cities or celebrated places where the services of skilled jurists and the testimony of experts, if required, might be had.[22]

The Fathers of the Council of Trent gave further stability to the reform of Boniface VIII by prescribing that in every provincial council or diocesan synod there should be chosen at least four judges for each diocese; and that the judges so selected should be endowed with the qualifications set forth by Boniface VIII and also with those natural and acquired facilities that would make them fitted for such an office; and that those selected should be called *Judices Synodales.* In the event of the death or resignation of one of these officers before the convocation of another synod the Ordinary with the consent of his chapter should appoint substitutes who would be called *Judices Pro-synodales.*[23]

The Council of Trent modified somewhat the former discipline of the Decretal Age in regard to criminal causes of the clergy by permitting a bishop or his delegate to proceed even to actual and solemn degradation of clerics, wherein the presence of bishops in specific number was required by the sacred canons, with a like number of abbots having the right by Apostolic privilege of using the mitre and crozier, or in the absence of these, assisted by a like number of other persons constituted in ecclesiastical dignity who were qualified by age and recommended by their knowledge.[24] Whether these assistants were judges with a decisive or only a consultative

[22] C. 11, *de rescriptis,* I, 3, in VI°.

[23] Conc. Trid., Sess. XXV, *de ref.,* c. 10.

[24] Conc. Trid., Sess. XIII, *de ref.,* c. 4.

vote is controverted. Molitor [25] seems to incline to the opinion that they were only "assessors" properly so called, that is, they acted simply as advisers to the judge and aided him to obtain a more complete knowledge of the case, and by their advice help him to decide justly. Heiner [26] holds that they had a decisive vote.

The Council also recommended that for all the more difficult causes, a bishop or his delegate should join to himself in very process at least two assessors who were to advise him. He was not bound to follow their advice. By common law these assessors had no jurisdiction but by particular law in some places they did possess jurisdiction, and in such cases they acted as associate judges and formed real collegiate tribunals.[27]

Unworthy and unqualified judges again found their way into the courts of the Church. Benedict XIV in his constitution *"Quamvis Paternae"* of August 26, 1741, found it necessary to reiterate the provisions of the Council of Trent, and to insist that in regions where synods were rarely convened, archbishops and bishops after consulting their chapters should select qualified judges and he imposed on them the obligation of registering the names of those appointed in the Roman Curia.[28]

The Age of the Decretals also saw the rise and origin of many Roman Congregations, Tribunals and Offices composed of several members and having judicial competence. They proceeded *per modum collegii* whenever they exercised this competence. Among them is the tribunal of the Sacred Roman Rota whose origin as a collegiate tribunal dates back to the first decades of the fourteenth century to the constitution *"Ratio Juris"* of John XXII.[29] The influence of this venerable tribunal depreciated in the centuries following the Reformation, but has since been reorganized and restored to its pristine splendor by Pius X in the constitution *"Sapienti Consilio"* of June 29, 1908.[30] How greatly the Regulae Servandae

[25] Molitor, *Ueber Kanonische Gerechtsverfahren gegen Cleriker*, p. 216.

[26] Heiner-Wynen, *De Processu Criminali*, p. 14.

[27] Conc. Trid., Sess. XXIV, *de ref.*, c. 10; Bouix, *De Judiciis Ecclesiasticis*, I, 467.

[28] *Fontes*, n. 315.

[29] Cerchiari, *Sacra Romana Rota*, III, 96 sq.

[30] *Fontes*, n. 682.

of this tribunal,[31] published August 4, 1910, have influenced the law of procedure for collegiate tribunals, can easily be seen from a study of the pertinent footnotes in the Gasparri edition of Codex Juris Canonici.

Art. III. Collegiate Tribunals in Particular Legislation of the Nineteenth Century

Beginning in the first half of the nineteenth century particular legislation of various dioceses prescribed the collegiate form of tribunal as the ordinary tribunal of first instance for hearing certain specified causes, on the ground that conclusions or decisions arrived at by several persons are of more weight and soundness than those reached by a single individual.

Gregory XVI set a notable example of this practice in the dioceses of the Papal states. In a circular letter sent out by the Papal Secretary of State dated November 4, 1831, he ordained that in every diocese of the Papal states there be set up as an ordinary tribunal for the adjudication of criminal causes of the clergy a court composed of the Ordinary and four clerical members and they were to hear and decide the cause by a majority vote.[32] In Rome the Court of the Vicariate consisted of the Cardinal Vicar and four prelates.[33] In a letter of April 24, 1832, the Secretary of State wrote that if on account of the smallness of the diocese it was impossible to obtain four such judges, at least two should be selected, and if this was not possible recourse to the Holy See was to be had in each case requiring the services of the court.[34] These letters had been ignored in certain places and the Congregation of Bishops and Regulars in a decree of March 1, 1851, again insisted that such a tribunal be established in every diocese.[35]

The Second Plenary Council of Baltimore[36] had enacted that a similar court composed of the Bishop or his Vicar-General and two priests selected by him should be used for criminal cases of clerics.

[31] *A.A.S.* II (1910), p. 783.
[32] Bizzarri, *Collectanea in Usum S.C.EE. et RR.*, p. 192 sq.
[33] Bouix, *De Iudiciis Ecclesiasticis*, I, 470.
[34] Bernasconii, *Acta Gregorii Papae XVI*, I, 66.
[35] *A.S.S.* XV, 547.
[36] *Concilii Plenarii Baltimorensis II, Acta et Decreta*, n. 77.

The Sacred Congregation of Propaganda on July 20, 1878, decreed that this tribunal should consist of five priests or, and where so many could not be had, at least three priests were to constitute a committee of investigation. These priests were to be selected by the Bishop in and with the advice of his synod, and the members were to hold office until the next synod. If a synod could not be held in the near future, three or five ecclesiastics as stated above were to be appointed by the Bishop. After investigating the case carefully and after a discussion on its merits, each member was to write out his opinion *in extenso* together with the reasons on which it was based. A majority vote was then required for the opinion of the court. This opinion together with the records of the case was then given to the Bishop who passed the final sentence.[37]

A similar tribunal was prescribed for England and the British Isles by the same Congregation in a decree of August 4, 1854, with this difference, that in England it was necessary that two-thirds of the judges instead of a bare majority should decide the opinion of the court.[38]

Among other documents which reflect this trend towards the collegiate tribunal as an ordinary tribunal of the diocesan curia is the *Instructio pro Judiciis Ecclesiasticis Imperii Austriaci quoad Causas Matrimoniales,* issued by Cardinal Rauscher for use in Austria and commonly known as "The Austrian Instruction." It bears the date of May 4, 1885. It prescribed that a collegiate tribunal of at least four and at the most six members selected by the Bishop hear the case. The decision of the tribunal was reached by an absolute majority of votes. The defender of the bond was to be heard. Before the tribunal gave sentence, the decision reached, and the motives upon which it was based were to be submitted to the Bishop who either approved it, or ordered a further examination. In case of a tie the presiding official decided the matter with his vote except when it was a question of the validity of the marriage. The validity of the marriage was to be upheld in the event of a tie vote.[39]

[37] *A.S.S.*, XIII, 324.

[38] *Collectio Lacensis,* III, 925-960.

[39] *Collectio Lacensis,* V, 1286 sq.

In the diocese of Spires in Germany the matrimonial causes were heard by a collegiate tribunal directed by the Vicar General with the defender of the bond in attendance.[40]

The Congregation of the Propagation of Faith issued an instruction on matrimonial procedure in the year 1883 in which it was stated that the judge, the Ordinary or his delegate was to have the opinion of two or three skilled consultors before pronouncing sentence.[41] A similar instruction was issued June 20, 1883, by the Holy Office to the Oriental Bishops with a few changes relative to special conditions obtaining in the East.[42]

Art. IV. The Development of Procedure in Matrimonial Causes

A short historical sketch of the development of procedure in matrimonial causes is added here. Attention is given only to those causes which demanded a formal trial. The history of the documentary process, and of causes involving the Pauline Privilege, and causes looking to a dispensation *super matrimonio rato et non consummato* is purposely excluded as not properly falling within the scope of this dissertation.

It can be considered as certain that even in the primitive Church the faithful did not decide for themselves the most important questions concerning marriage.[43] If there are not many recorded cases of judgment exercised by the Church, this is accounted for by the fact that in those times, there were few diriment impediments. There is evidence that individual bishops treated matrimonial causes in diocesan synods,[44] and that provincial councils served as tribunals for matrimonial causes.[45] Steps in appeal were generally from the

[40] Roskovany, *Matrimonium*, III, p. 110.

[41] *Collectanea Sacrae Congregationis de Propaganda Fide*, n. 1587.

[42] *Fontes*, n. 1076.

[43] I Cor. V, 1 sq.; Ignatius M., *Ep. ad Polycarp*. c. 5—Lightfoot, *Apostolic Fathers*, II, 347, 573; Justin, *Apologia* II, n. 2—*MPG*, VI, 443.

[44] C. of Ancyre (314), c. 24—Mansi II, 522; C. of Vannes (465), c. 2—Mansi VII, 953; C. of Agatha (506), c. 25—Mansi, VIII, 329.

[45] C. 10, C. XXXV, q. 6; c. 1, C. XXXIII, q. 2; Hincmar's account of the Synod of Tousy II (860)—Mansi, XV, 571; Perrone, *De Matrimonio Christiano*, II, 351.

bishop and his synod, or from the provincial council to the Holy See.

From the eighth century on, documentary evidence that the Church exercised her judgment in matrimonial causes becomes more plentiful. Gratian declares that the adjudication of a marriage belongs to the tribunals of the Church.[46]

Popes Alexander II (1061),[47] Alexander III (1159-1181),[48] Lucius III (1181-1185),[49] Clement III (1187-1191),[50] leave no doubt in their decretals as to the competence of the Church in matrimonial causes. Matrimonial causes were conducted generally with all the legal formality of a solemn trial. Clement V (1310-1317) in two constitutions *"Dispendiosam"* [51] and *"Saepe"* [52] inaugurated a new summary judicial process which dispensed with the minutiae of the solemn forensic procedure but without sacrificing necessary proofs or precluding legitimate defense. These merely permitted the omission of some accidental requirements.

With the growth and spread of the Church litigation increased. The Bishops finding themselves overburdened with judicial business inaugurated the delegated courts of archdeacons, deans, archpriests and prelates of inferior rank. From about the twelfth century on these came to regard their jurisdiction as ordinary and their courts as courts of first instance with appeal from their court to the court of the Bishop. A considerable part of their work concerned matrimonial causes. The manner in which these inferior courts exercised jurisdiction in matrimonial affairs was a constant source of complaint from the time of Innocent III (1198-1216) to the Council of Trent. Abuses prevailed almost universally. Frequently the judges lacked the necessary knowledge and skill requisite for their office.[53]

The struggle to curb the power of these inferior prelates extended

[46] Cc. 1, 3, 4, C. XXXIII, q. 2.

[47] C. 10, C. XXXV, q. 6.

[48] C. 3, X, *de divortiis,* IV, 19.

[49] C. 10, X, *de restitutione spoliatorum,* II, 13.

[50] C. 13, I, *de restitutione spoliatorum,* II, 13.

[51] C. 2, *de judiciis,* II, I in Clem.

[52] C. 2, *de verborum significatione,* V, II, in Clem.

[53] C. 1, X, *de lite non contestata,* II, 6; C. of York (1387) C. 8—Mansi, XXVI, 468.

over centuries. The IV Lateran Council (1215) found it necessary to warn inferior prelates especially abbots to leave matrimonial causes to the care of the Bishops.[54] Innocent III (1198-1216) complained of these courts.[55] Legislation was introduced in various synods as early as the thirteenth century to restrict their jurisdiction. The Synod of Poitiers (1280) [56] required a special mandate before they could sit in judgment on causes. In some places excommunication was threatened for inferior prelates who presumed to decide matrimonial causes.[57] Finally the Council of Trent (1553) provided that all matrimonial and criminal causes should be henceforth brought before the Bishop.[58]

After the Council of Trent there was no longer any wavering as to the jurisdiction of the Bishop. Archdeacons, deans and other inferior prelates were deprived of their competence in matrimonial causes. The court of the Bishop was the court of first instance, with the tribunal of the metropolitan as the court of appeal. Even nuncios and legates of the Holy See were forbidden to interfere with the exercise of the bishops' authority. Excepted from this general rule were those causes which were reserved by law to the Holy See, and those which for urgent and special reasons were withdrawn by the Pope from episcopal competence. These causes were tried by judges delegated for this purpose by the Holy See. The concern and anxiety of the Popes and councils that this delegated power might be exercised by worthy and qualified judges is seen in the legislation enacted by Boniface VIII,[59] the Council of Trent,[60] and Benedict XIV.[61]

Benedict XIV in a constitution *"Dei miseratione"* of November 3, 1741, introduced a sweeping reform in matrimonial proce-

[54] Mansi, XXII, 1047.

[55] C. 1, X, *de lite non contestata,* II, 6.

[56] Mansi, XXIV, 382.

[57] C. of York (1367), c. 8—Mansi, XXV, 277.

[58] Sess. XXIV, *de ref.,* c. 20.

[59] C. 11, *de rescriptis* I, 3, in VI°; c. 15, *de officio et potestate judicis delegati,* I, 14, in VI°.

[60] Conc. Trid., Sess. XXV, *de ref.,* c. 10.

[61] Cf. Ep ency. *Quamvis Paternae,* Aug. 26, 1741.—*Fontes,* n. 315.

dure.[62] In a preamble the great Pontiff deplores the facility and haste with which marriages were being pronounced invalid in ecclesiastical courts, and the scandal thus given. Next he enumerates the causes of this abuse. Certain ecclesiastical judges pronounce marriages invalid upon slight or no investigation. Frequently only the party demanding the nullity appeared at the trial, the other failing to appear and defend the marriage. Collusion on the part of the parties for the purpose of having their marriage declared invalid was not infrequent. To remedy these grave evils, Benedict XIV obliged every Bishop of the world to appoint in his diocese a defender of the bond.[63] This defender was to be regarded as so necessary in all cases where there was a question of the validity or nullity of marriage, that is, in all cases where there was a question of annulling a marriage already contracted, he must be cited for every judicial act, and unless he was cited any act whatsoever of the court to which he was not called was of no effect whatever.[64] He enacted that two conformable sentences were required on the invalidity of a marriage before the parties could enter a new union; that matrimonial causes of nullity never became *res judicatae;* that even if a marriage had been twice declared invalid and the parties had remarried, it was allowed at any time afterwards to produce new proofs to show that the marriage was valid.[65] The only exception was, where both parties were dead, and a long time afterwards the legitimacy of their children was impugned on the ground that the parents' marriage was invalid.

If the first sentence was for the invalidity of the marriage, the defender of the bond was bound to appeal even though the party against whom the sentence was pronounced did not wish to appeal. If the court of second instance like the first, pronounced a marriage invalid he need not appeal unless the sentence seemed manifestly unjust or invalid. If the sentence of first instance was for the validity and this decision was reversed in the second instance, the defender was found to appeal to a third instance.

[62] *Fontes,* n. 318.
[63] Const., *Dei miseratione* §5.
[64] Const., *Dei miseratione* §5.
[65] Const., *Dei miseratione* §11.

The grades of appeal were established as follows. The local ordinary was the court of first instance, with the tribunal of the metropolitan, papal nuncio, neighboring bishop or delegated judge as the court of second instance.[66] The Holy See was ordinarily the court of third instance, but the faithful might use the Holy See as the tribunal of either first, second or third instance.

Matrimonial causes involving the impediment of impotence were tried in diocesan tribunals. This impediment has always been difficult to establish, and frequently a Papal dispensation *super matrimonio rato et non consummato* was asked. An instruction came from the Holy Office in 1858 relative to the procedure to be observed in such cases entitled "Pro conficiendo processu super viri impotentia, et non secuta matrimonii consummatione, accedenti Pontificis dispensatione ab accurata observantia praescriptionum Bullae Benedicti XIV, Dei miseratione."[67] Another instruction of the same Congregation issued in 1868 outlined the procedure to be followed in proving the death of a spouse.[68]

The legislation of Benedict XIV, and of the Roman Congregations, which has enduring value was supplemented later, especially in the middle nineteenth century by instructions from Rome of a far reaching nature, and also by individual decrees. As pertinent to the subject of this dissertation mention is made here of an instruction of the Sacred Congregation of Council dated August 22, 1840, in which it was decreed that the prescriptions of Benedict XIV in the constitution *"Dei miseratione"* must be observed under penalty of the invalidity of all the judicial acts; that the bishop was the ordinary judge and should himself or through a delegated judge, not only pronounce sentence but even preside at the trial; that the absence of the defender in cases in which his presence was required would invalidate the acts of the court. Appeals were to be made according to the directions of the constitution *"Dei miseratione,"* and the bishop was to send an authentic copy of the acts to the judge of second instance.[69]

[66] Const., *Dei miseratione* §10.

[67] S. C. S. Off., Instr., 1858—*Fontes*, n. 946.

[68] S. C. S. Off., Instr., 1868—*Fontes*, n. 1002.

[69] S. C. C. Inst., Aug. 22, 1840—*Coll.*, n. 911.

An instruction of the Congregation de Propaganda Fide to the Bishops of the United States in 1883 [70] prescribed a special form of procedure for matrimonial processes. This instruction to the American bishops speaks of the bishop, the vicar general or approved delegate as the moderator of the acts. The judge, whether he was the ordinary or his delegate, was to have the advice of two or three skilled consultors before pronouncing sentence. Two conformable sentences were required before the parties could marry again, and not even then if the defender of the bond appealed the case. They were obliged to await decision on the appeal. If the first sentence declared the invalidity of the marriage the defender of the bond was obliged to appeal; but if the first sentence affirmed the validity the defender was not obliged to take the matter to a higher court but the parties could appeal. The metropolitan court was the court of second instance and Rome was ordinarily the court of third instance. If a metropolitan court was the tribunal of first instance, a nearby metropolitan tribunal was to be chosen as a court of second instance. Causes could be introduced at Roman tribunals as courts of first instance. A similar instruction had been issued by the Holy Office to the Oriental Bishops a short time before wherein special provisions were made for conditions in the East. Appeal in the Eastern Church was from the Bishop to the Patriarch. If the Patriarch had tried the case in the first instance appeal was to be made to the Holy See. Orientals also had the privilege of introducing marriage causes directly at the Holy See.[71]

The Code of Canon Law effective May 19, 1918, codified all of the former legislation which still governs matrimonial procedure devoting Title XX of Book IV to this subject.

[70] *Coll.*, n. 1587.

[71] S. C. S. Off., Inst. (ad Ep. Rituum Orient.) June 20, 1883—*Fontes*, 1076.

PART II

THE PRESENT LEGISLATION

CHAPTER II

THE CONSTITUTION OF THE DIOCESAN COLLEGIATE TRIBUNAL OF THE COURT OF FIRST INSTANCE

ART. I. THE NECESSITY OF THE COLLEGIATE TRIBUNAL

THE first canon of Title II in Book IV of the Code lays down this general principle of Canon Law, that in every diocese and for all causes not expressly exempted by law the local Ordinary is the judge of first instance.[1]

Causes Exempted by Law. The Holy See can be judged by no one.[2] The Roman Pontiff reserves to himself exclusively the right to judge the causes of the following persons: 1. All causes of those who hold the highest governmental rank in a nation, and their sons and daughters and those who have immediate right of succession.[3] This includes that ruler, man or woman, who holds the supreme authority of the people, their legitimate sons and daughters, and stepchildren,[4] and those next in the right of succession. Presidents and any other potentate who is a supreme magistrate in a republic, as long as they actually are in power are included also. Some are inclined to the opinion that the cause of a president-elect of the United States prior to his inauguration would come under this canon because he has the right of succession in office.[5] While the vice-president of the United States is included in this category because he would succeed to the presidency in case it was vacated, his wife or family are not included.

In view of the fact that by the Constitution of the United States each state of the Union is sovereign, and legislates for itself, it seems that the reservation contained in this canon might reasonably be extended to include the governors of states and their families, and the lieutenant-governor.

[1] Can. 1572, §1.

[2] Can. 1556.

[3] Can. 1557, §1.

[4] Blat, *Commentarium* IV, n. 12.

[5] Wernz-Vidal, *Jus Canonicum,* VI, n. 49.

2. All causes of cardinals, contentious as well as criminal,[6] from the moment the Pope creates them and publishes their names in a secret consistory.[7]

3. Contentious as well as criminal causes of any Legate of the Apostolic See—Nuncios, Internuncios and Apostolic Delegates, and the criminal causes of all Bishops residential as well as titular,[8] from the moment they have received authentic notice of the promotion.[9]

To the tribunals of the Holy See are reserved judgment over the following:

1. Contentious causes of residential bishops with the exception of those causes mentioned in Canon 1572, §2, n. 1, which are to be judged, by a tribunal composed of the official as praeses and two senior synodal judges, if the bishop consents, or by the metropolitan.

2. Dioceses and other ecclesiastical persons who have no superior below the Supreme Pontiff, such as exempt religious organizations and monastic congregations.[10]

Other causes which the Roman Pontiff cites to his tribunal shall be judged by the judge whom the Roman Pontiff himself shall have appointed.[11]

The causes mentioned above are reserved in such a manner that all other judges are absolutely incompetent.[12] Everyone else is excluded absolutely, even a preliminary hearing or taking cognizance of the case being forbidden, and an attempted sentence would be *ipso jure* invalid.

Other causes removed from the competence of the local Ordinary are those reserved by law to any superior tribunal or those brought directly to the Holy See.[13]

Causes arising from disputes between individual religious of the

[6] Can. 1557, §1, n. 2.
[7] Can. 233, §1.
[8] Can. 1557, §1.
[9] Can. 349, §1.
[10] Can. 1572, §2, n. 2.
[11] Can. 1572, §3.
[12] Can. 1558.
[13] Can. 1569, §1.

same exempt clerical organization, or between two Provinces, or between two autonomous monasteries are also removed from the competence of the Bishop.[14]

If a controversy arises between physical or moral persons of different religious organizations or between individual religious of non-exempt congregations or lay institutes or between a religious and a secular cleric or a lay person the local Ordinary is the judge of the first instance.[15]

While the Bishop is the judge in a diocese, the Code advises that this office be performed generally through others.[16] Each bishop is held to select an Official distinct from the Vicar General.[17] The Official has ordinary power and constitutes one tribunal with the Bishop and there is no appeal from the Official to the Bishop.[18]

Besides the court wherein the Official presides as a judge sole the Code demands that there be set up in every diocese as an ordinary court of first instance, a collegiate tribunal composed of the Official and two or four synodal judges, who meet and act as a body, and decide cases referred to them according to the prescriptions of the sacred canons. The obligation of setting up this tribunal is absolute, is obligatory in every diocese, abbey and prelature *nullius*.[19] Every contrary custom is and should be amended as a corruption of the law even though it be immemorial.[20] A contrary custom arising in the future is to be considered as unreasonable, and therefore cannot produce the effect of a law.[21] Any contrary privilege enjoyed by physical or moral persons prior to the Code is revoked.[22] But any agreement entered into between the Holy See and different nations affecting this question remains in full force notwithstanding this contrary prescription of the Code.[23]

[14] Can. 1579, §1.
[15] Can. 1579, §3.
[16] Can. 1578.
[17] Can. 1573, §1.
[18] Can. 1573, §2.
[19] Cans. 1576, §1, and 215, §2.
[20] Can. 5.
[21] Can. 27.
[22] Can. 4.
[23] Can. 3.

Art. II. Composition of the Collegiate Tribunal

Ordinarily, the collegiate tribunal of the diocesan court of first instance is composed of the official or the vice-official and two or four synodal or pro-synodal judges, accordingly as the Sacred Canons permit or prescribed three or five judges for the hearing of certain causes.[24]

A. *The Office of the Official.* It was commonly accepted by authors following Thomassinus, prior to the year 1922 that the origin of the office of the Official could be traced to the efforts of the Bishops of the thirteenth and fourteenth centuries to curb the influence of the inferior prelates particularly the archdeacons, and that the office in the course of time was absorbed by that of the Vicar General.[25] It was first established that this fusion of offices took place only in the smaller dioceses of Italy, and that in France, England and Germany the offices of Vicar General and Official were always distinct.[26] In 1922 Edouard Fournier,[27] and after him Erwin von Kienitz [28] in 1931 asserted, and have substantiated with documentary proof, that the origin of the office of the Official must be traced to the necessities of the times rather than to the struggles between the bishops and the archdeacons. Even before the twelfth century the burden of litigation in the courts of the bishops increased tremendously owing to the various collections of laws compiled for the use and government of the clergy and the faithful.[29] There arose a necessity for the services of men expert in law, who might relieve the Bishops of a large part of their judicial work. To this fact do Fournier and von Kienitz attribute the origin of the Official.

Long before the struggle between the Bishops and the Archdea-

[24] Cans. 1572, §2; 1576, §1, n. 2; 1576, §2.

[25] Thomassinus, *Vetera et Nova Ecclesiae Disciplinae circa Beneficia et Beneficiarios*, P. I, Lib. II, cap. VIII.

[26] Schalz, *De Instituto Officialis sive Vicarii Generalis Episcopi*, n. 78; Fournier, Ed., *Les origines du Vicaire General;* Hinchius, *System des Katholischen Kircherechts*, pp. 205-227.

[27] Fournier, *Les origines du Vicar General*, p. 22 sq.

[28] Van Kienitz, *General vikar und Offizial*, p. 13 sq.

[29] Cf. Van Hove, *Prolegomena*, p. 138.

cons became acute, various councils as early as the ninth century speak of the Official as the *judex episcopi* who participated in the contentious rather than the voluntary jurisdiction of the Bishops.[30]

From the fourteenth century the evidence for the existence of the Official as a diocesan judge cannot be doubted.[31] He constituted one tribunal with the Bishop, and appeal from the court of the Official to the Bishop was impossible. It seems that the present law of separating the offices of the Vicar General and the Official is merely a return to the ancient discipline.

Canon 1573, § 1. Quilibet Episcopus tenetur Officialem eligere cum potestate ordinaria iudicandi, a Vicario Generali distinctum, nisi parvitas dioecesis aut paucitas negotiorum suadeat hoc officium ipsi Vicario Generali committi.

The present legislation decrees that the Bishop is held to appoint an Official in every diocese. Under the term *Episcopus,* both the Abbot and the prelate *nullius* are included.[32] Vicars and Prefects Apostolic may appoint an Official in their territories if the amount of judicial work warrants it and the member of the clergy permits it.[33] He should be distinct from the Vicar General. But if, because of the smallness of the diocese or because of the rare occurrence of judicial trials there is little need for the services of an Official, the office of Vicar General and Official may be held by the same individual.[34]

1. *Appointment of Official.* The Official is appointed by the Bishop without the concurrence of anyone. Abbots and prelates *nullius* appoint the Official in their respective territories.[35] The

[30] C. of Paris (1213), Par. IV—Mansi XXII, 841; C. of Rouen (1189), cc. 8, 13, 27—Mansi XXII, 525; C. of Canterbury (1295), cap. IV—Mansi XXII, 1149; C. of Turin (1239), cc. 13, 22, 28—Mansi XXIII, 412.

[31] C. 2, *de officio vicarii,* I, 14, in VI°.

[32] Can. 215.

[33] Vromant: Jus Missionariorum, II, n. 79. Vermeersch-Creusen—*Epitome,* I, n. 369.

[34] Can. 1573, §1.

[35] Can. 215, §2.

Vicar General cannot appoint the Official without a special mandate of the Bishop. During the vacancy of a diocese he may be appointed by the Vicar Capitular on Administrator.[36] If the Official is appointed Vicar Capitular or Administrator during the vacancy of a See he must appoint a new Official.[37] If a Vicar General is at the same time Official, the office of Vicar General ceases with the vacancy of the See but the office of Official does not.[38] Assistants may be assigned to the Official with the title of Vice Officials.[39]

The appointment should be made in writing.[40] Before entering upon this office they should make the Profession of Faith according to the formula of Pius IV and Pius IX as given in the beginning of the Code, and take the oath against modernism, according to the formula contained in the Motu Proprio "Sacrorum Antistitum" of Pius X September 1, 1910,[41] and the oath *"de munere fideliter exercendo et secreto servando."*[42]

2. *Qualities of the Official and Vice-official.* They must be priests of irreproachable reputation. Hence those guilty of the crimes mentioned in Canons 2353, 2263, 2375, 2385 are *ipso jure* prohibited from holding this office. Those mentioned in Canons 2294, §2; 2256, §2; 2315, 2352, 2357, §2, are to be expelled from this office. All those who are forbidden the legitimate ecclesiastical acts [43] or those who have incurred a penalty which carries with it the prohibition of exercising such acts, as suspension from office [44] or from jurisdiction [45] or have incurred *infamia juris* [46] or deposition [47] or degradation [48] cannot validly exercise this office after a condemnatory or declaratory sentence.

36 Cans. 198, 391, 431, 432, 437.
37 Can. 1573, §7.
38 Can. 1573, §6.
39 Can. 1573, §3.
40 Cans. 159, 364, §1.
41 Can. 1406, §1, n. 7; *A.A.S.* II (1910); *Periodica,* V (1913), 200.
42 Can. 364, §1.
43 Cfr. Can. 2256, §2.
44 Can. 2279, §1.
45 Can. 2279, §2, n. 1.
46 Can. 2294, §1.
47 Can. 2303, §1.
48 Can. 2305, §1.

They should possess the degree of Doctor of Canon Law, or at least have a thorough knowledge of Canon Law, and be at least thirty years of age.[49]

Canon 153 declares that a cleric who is appointed to any given office should possess the qualities required by law, and his fitness may be tested by an examination. Attention might also be called to Canon 157 which prohibits the collation of any office upon *familiares* or close relatives of the person who is conferring the office, or of the person who resigned or was deprived of an office.

Can a religious be appointed Official in a diocese not committed exclusively to the care of religious? The Code does not give a direct or definite answer. Canon 626, §1, merely says that a religious cannot be appointed to any office that is incompatible with the religious state. It seems that the spirit of the law is against such an appointment. They are excluded from the office of Vicar General unless the diocese is entrusted to the Order. Religious may not act as notaries in ecclesiastical trials, not even in causes of beatification except by necessity.[50] They are forbidden to act as advocates or procurators in tribunals outside of a religious community.[51] So it seems logical to infer that a religious cannot be appointed Official.[52] A secularized religious is likewise prohibited from holding this office.[53]

3. *Nature and Extent of the Power of the Official.* The power of the Official is ordinary.[54] So too is the power of the Vice-Officials [55] when they act as substitutes for the Official. It is not expedient that both function in the same cause.

The court of the Official is to be considered as one and the same grade with that of the Bishop, and no appeal is possible from the court of the Official to that of the Bishop.[56] The Bishop

[49] Can. 1572, §4.

[50] Can. 2014.

[51] Can. 1657.

[52] Can. 626, §1; Noval, *De Processibus*, n. 116; Roberti, *De Processibus*, I, n. 98.

[53] Can. 642.

[54] Can. 197, §1.

[55] De Angelo, *La Curia Diocesana*, I, 161.

[56] Can. 1573, §2.

may limit the jurisdiction of the Official by reserving cases to himself, but he should not make these reservations so numerous as to change the character of his power or to make the Official for practical purposes, a delegated rather than an ordinary judge.

4. *Removal.* The Official and the Vice-Officials are removable *ad nutum episcopi* for any reasonable cause. The Bishop is not obliged to reveal his reasons.[57] The Official continues in office even though the episcopal see is vacant. He cannot be removed from office by the Vicar Capitular or Administrator [58] except for a crime, and then only for a crime for which he has been convicted through judicial procedure. The Vicar Capitular or Administrator may however suspend from office for a just cause the Official according to the provisions of Canon 2222. The Official must look for confirmation in office to the new bishop when he comes into office. This ratification may be expressed or tacit and the Official may validly continue to exercise his office until he is removed by the new Bishop.

An Official may resign. Apart from a specific prohibition of law anyone may resign an office, but to be valid, it must be an act that is free from unjust fear, error, etc.; [59] it must be made in writing or before two witnesses; [60] and must be accepted by a competent superior.[61] In this case the competent superior would be the Bishop, Abbot or Prelate *Nullius*, the Vicar Capitular, or Administrator. A resignation does not take effect, until the one resigning is notified that the resignation has been accepted by the competent superior.[62]

B. *Synodal and Pro-synodal Judges.* Synodal judges had their origin in the middle ages when the Holy See, because of the multiplicity of cases referred to it from afar, found it necessary to assign these cases to delegated judges, to be adjudged in places outside of Rome. It frequently happened, because the Holy See knew little or

[57] Can. 1573, §5.

[58] Can. 1573, §2, n. 5; C. 436. Noval, *De Processibus*, p. 116.

[59] Can. 185.

[60] Can. 186.

[61] Can. 187.

[62] Can. 190.

nothing concerning the persons who enjoyed Papal jurisdiction, that unworthy and unqualified judges were in possession of this delegated power. In order that the Holy See might be represented by worthy and capable persons, Boniface VIII decreed that in the future no one might fulfill the office of delegated judge, unless "he was a canon of a cathedral church, or was endowed with an ecclesiastical dignity, or possessed of a personate." [63]

Later the Council of Trent prescribed, that in every provincial or diocesan synod there should be chosen at least four such judges for each diocese, that the judges so selected should be endowed with the qualifications set forth by Boniface VIII in the constitution *"Statuimus,"* [63a] and also with those natural and acquired qualities as would fit them for such an office. They should be called *judices synodales*. In case of the death of any of these before the convocation of a new synod, the Ordinary with the consent of his chapter should appoint substitutes who would be called *judices pro-synodales*.[64] Benedict XIV in his constitution *"Quamvis Paternae"* of August 26, 1741, reiterated the provisions of the Council of Trent and further decreed that in those regions where synods were rarely convened, the Bishops should select these judges and register their names in the Roman Curia.[65]

Synodal judges did not possess a permanent and constant function. They were merely qualified and approved judges to whom the Holy See might with confidence entrust for decision judicial matters which were referred to her forum.

1. *Qualifications*. In the present legislation synodal judges have only the name in common with synodal judges of former times. They are no longer officers of the Holy See but diocesan judges appointed by the Bishop at the time of the diocesan synod to act as judges when so delegated by the Bishop, and to form with the Official or the Bishop, the ordinary collegiate tribunal of the diocesan

[63] C. 11, *de rescriptis*, I, 3, in VI°; c. 20, *de hereticis*, V, 2, in VI°.
[63a] C. 11, *de rescriptis*, I, 3, in VI°.
[64] Conc. Trid., Sess. XXV, *de ref.*, c. 10.
[65] *Fontes*, n. 315.

curia. They may also be assumed by a judge sole to act as assessors or counselors in every trial.[66]

In the present law of the Church, synodal judges need not have those qualifications demanded by the law of the Decretals, according to which they were to be men constituted in ecclesiastical dignity or in a personate, or canons of the cathedral church. The Code requires but three qualifications: 1. That they be priests. Blat [67] regards the word *sacerdotes* as taxative and excludes titular Bishops. They may be priests of another diocese. 2. They must be men of unblemished character. What has been said relative to the moral character of the Official must be applied to synodal judges.[68] 3. They should be experts in Canon Law.[69]

Noval [70] would exclude religious from the office of synodal judge claiming the office is incompatible with their state of life. Roberti with others [71] would permit religious to be synodal judges, claiming that this office is compatible with religious life. He appeals to the practice of the Vicariate of Rome where religious are used as synodal and pro-synodal judges.

2. *Election and Substitution of Synodal Judges.* Synodal judges are to be chosen in the diocesan synod according to the rules of Canon Law contained in Canon 385. The Code fixes the maximum and minimum number for each diocese. There shall be not more than twelve and not less than four. The smallest necessary number of judges is four because in certain canonical trials a tribunal composed of the Official and four synodal judges is required.[72] It is left to the prudent judgment of the Bishop to determine how many more than the minimum number are required for the necessities of his diocese. In fixing this number he should give consideration to the amount of work to be done by the tribunal, the labor entailed in

[66] Cans. 1575; 1940, §1; 2040.

[67] *De Processibus*, p. 45.

[68] Cfr. p. ....

[69] Can. 1574, §1.

[70] *De Processibus*, n. 118.

[71] Roberti, n. 112; Cocchi, *De Processibus*, n. 19; Schäfer, *De Religiosis*, n. 493; Maroto, *Apollinaris* (1931), annus IV, num. 2, p. 252.

[72] Can. 1576, §1, n. 2.

examining documents and witnesses, and the contingencies of sickness, absence from the diocese, vacations and the duties incumbent on the judges from other labors in which they are engaged.

Synodal judges are usually chosen in the first solemn session of the synod. The Bishop proposes the names and they are approved by the consent of the majority of the synod.[73] This may be done in various ways. A very convenient way is to have the list made up in the form of printed ballots with space along side each name for the *placet* or *non placet* of the voters. It might be well to allow for freedom of choice by adding several extra names. The tellers are appointed, two in number. The ballots are distributed one to each member present. The voters will write a cross beside the names of those whom they wish to elect. When the voting is finished the ballots are collected and given to the Bishop, who in turn presents them to the tellers. They will proceed to open them and record the votes. A majority vote is required for those chosen but a relative majority will suffice after the second ballot.[74] If one or the other candidate or all the candidates proposed by the Bishop do not receive the necessary majority, the Bishop must propose other names for those rejected until the necessary number of judges has been reached.[75] The names of those chosen are usually announced in the same session.

3. *Substitution.* The tenure of office for a synodal judge is ten years unless another synod is held before the expiration of that time, when the term of office automatically expires.[76] If a synodal judge should die or go out of office during the time intervening between synods, the Bishop with the advice of the chapter or diocesan consultors shall appoint another in his stead and he shall be called a pro-synodal judge.[77] The priest appointed to fill the unexpired term of a synodal judge, stays in office for the remaining part of that

[73] Vromant, *Jus Missionariorum,* II, 205, Oesterle, *Praelectiones Juris Canonici,* I, 189; Vermeersch-Creusen, *Epitome,* II, n. 445; Blat, *Commentarium,* II, n. 423.

[74] Can. 101, §1, n. 1.

[75] Benedict XIV, *De Synodo Dioecesana* I. IV, c. 7, n. 2.

[76] Cans. 387, 1574, §2.

[77] Can. 386.

term.[78] If a synod is not held in a diocese an obligation rests on the Bishop of selecting with the advice of the Chapter or the consultors the requisite number of judges who shall be called pro-synodal judges and they shall hold office for ten years unless a synod is held in the meantime.[79] A synodal judge or a pro-synodal judge may be reelected indefinitely.[80]

The appointment of synodal and pro-synodal judges should be reduced to writing. Before entering upon their office they should make the Profession of Faith and take the oath against modernism and the oath *de munere fideliter exercendo et secreto servando*.[81]

In virtue of Canon 387 the judges may finish any cause they have begun to hear, and which remains unfinished at the time of the expiration of their term of office. The words *"negotium jam coeptum"* of Canon 387 are to be understood, after the citation of the defendant has been properly made, because only then can a tribunal lawfully proceed to summon witnesses, receive proofs, depositions and reports of experts, etc.[82]

4. *Removal of Synodal and Pro-Synodal Judges.* Synodal and pro-synodal judges can be removed from office only for a grave cause and with the advice of the cathedral chapter or diocesan consultors.[83] Only the advice and not the consent of the chapter or the consultors is required. Hence removal without the consent of the chapter or the consultors would be valid.

A grave cause would be a reason sufficient for removing a pastor, or a crime which admits of or demands removal from office according to the penal code. Moreover, for any violation of their oath to keep the secret of office[84] the Bishop must remove synodal and pro-synodal judges from office and he is therefore not at liberty to apply or not apply this penal sanction. As soon as the violation is proved

[78] Can. 387, §2.

[79] Cans. 386, 1574, §1.

[80] Can. 385.

[81] Can. 364, §1; cf. *Sacrorum Antistitum, A.A.S.*, II, (1910) 669; *Periodica*, V, (1913), 200.

[82] Can. 1725.

[83] Can. 388.

[84] Can. 1625, §2.

or as soon as the Bishop is morally certain that a judge has revealed the secret, he must remove him. No formal procedure is required. The Vicar Capitular or the Administrator cannot remove a synodal or pro-synodal judge except with the consent of the chapter or the diocesan consultors and for a crime and then only for a crime for which he has been convicted through judicial procedure,[85] and which carries with it deprivation of office. The Vicar Capitular or Administrator may, however, suspend synodal or pro-synodal judges according to the provisions of Canon 2222. A synodal or pro-synodal judge may resign for any valid reason, provided the resignation is properly executed and accepted by the competent superior. Valid reasons would be advanced age, sickness, consciousness of a crime, entrance and profession in a religious order. It takes effect when he has been notified of the acceptance of the resignation.[86] The law also admits besides this express or explicit resignation a tacit resignation which is brought about and signified by a fact, upon which the law itself has decreed the loss of office.[87]

Must the advice *"de consilio Capituli cathedralis"* or *"de consilio consultorum"* which the Bishop is directed to seek according to Canon 386, §1, in selecting pro-synodal judges or by Canon 388 in removing either synodal or pro-synodal judges, be sought for the validity of the appointment or the removal? The question is controverted, and hinges on the interpretation that is to be placed on Canon 105, §1.

The opinion of Vermeersch, Creusen, Boudinhon, and Vromant does not require that a bishop seek the advice of his chapter or consultors under penalty of the invalidity of the appointment or removal of synodal or pro-synodal judges.[88]

The more common opinion espoused by such canonists as Ojetti, Chelodi, Maroto, Cocchi, Ferreres, De Meester, Blat, Toso, Coro-

[85] Cans. 373, §5, 2281.

[86] Cans. 183; 187.

[87] Can. 188.

[88] Vermeersch, *Epitome* I, n. 197 bis.; Creusen, "L'effet juridique des consultations," *N.R.T.*, LV[1], 1928, p. 100 sq.; Boudinhon, *Jus Pontificium VIII* (1928), p. 29 sq.; Vromant, *De Bonis Ecclesiae Temporalibus*, n. 40; Wernz-Vidal, *Jus Canonicum*, II, n. 33, p. 35.

nata, Leitner, is that a bishop must seek the advice of the chapter or consultors for the validity of these appointments or removals.[89]

Until such time as an authentic interpretation is given on this canon, since the less common opinion has at least extrinsic probability, it can be safely followed, and acts executed in violation of Canon 105, §1, by virtue of Canons 11 and 15 may be considered valid. However, it is absolutely foreign to the mind of the legislator that Canon 11 or any other canon should lend encouragement to the non-observance or disregard of such prescriptions in the law.

As was stated before in this chapter not less than four and not more than twelve synodal or pro-synodal judges are to be selected for every diocese, who shall be delegated by the Bishop to form with the Official the ordinary collegiate tribunal of the diocesan curia. The *praeses* of every *turnus* of this tribunal is the Official or the Vice-Official. The associate judges sit in turns of two or four in number with the Official accordingly as the Code demands or permits a tribunal of three or five judges. They may be chosen to sit for one or more causes at a time, or in a certain class of causes or *ad universitatem causarum*. But unless the Ordinary decrees otherwise, they shall function in boards of two or four judges with the Official in the cases assigned to that particular board by the Ordinary.[90] The Ordinary may validly give to the Official the faculty of forming from these judges already constituted in office the various boards. These various boards of judges constitute so many available sections of the same tribunal and each section when functioning acts as a tribunal.

[89] Ojetti, *Commentarium in Codicem,* II, p. 186 sq.; Chelodi, *Jus De Personis,* n. 208; Maroto, *Institutiones Juris Canonici,* I, n. 471; Cocchi, *Commentarium in Codicem Juris Canonici,* lib. II, P.I., Sect. II, n. 11; Ferreres, *Institutiones Canonici* I, n. 229; De Meester, *Juris Canonici et Juris Canonico-civilis Compendium II,* n. 879; Blat, *Commentarium,* II, n. 36-526; Toso, *Commentaria Minora,* lib. II, P.I., Tit. I, p. 54; Coronata, *Institutiones Juris Canonici* I, n. 153; Leitner, *Handbuch des Katholischen Kirchenrechts* I, ed. II, p. 77.

[90] Can. 1574, §1.

C. *The Auxiliary Members of the Collegiate Tribunal.*

Besides the Official and the synodal judges, there are various other persons who may or who usually do intervene or assist the collegiate tribunal in conducting an ecclesiastical trial. Such are the Auditor, the Notary, the Defender of the Bond, the Promoter of Justice, Procurators, Advocates, Messengers and Interpreters. Consideration shall be given in this article only to the rights and duties of the Auditor. The duties of the Defender of the Bond, the Promoter of Justice and the Notary will be treated in Part Three, Chapter VI.[91] Reference shall be made in various places in the dissertation to the duties of the Procurators, Advocates, Messengers and Interpreters, without devoting separate articles to each of these officers.

The Auditor. An auditor may be defined as a cleric, who by reason of jurisdiction delegated to him, is empowered to summon parties and witnesses before an ecclesiastical court, to examine and otherwise hear their testimony, and to perform other judicial acts which fall within the limits of the commission through which he acts. D'Angelo is of the opinion that a layman might be appointed auditor provided he act merely as an *instructor actorum* or as a legal advisor. He could not be given jurisdiction.[92] Auditors have jurisdiction as far as the hearing or taking cognizance of the case is concerned but have no jurisdiction as to the final sentence.[93]

The appointment of auditors is optional. Their work may be done by the judges of the tribunal. The Code considers them as distinct from the judges of the collegiate tribunal, but there is nothing to prevent the *ponens* of the collegiate tribunal from assuming the duties of the auditor, at least in contentious causes.[94]

Auditors should as far as possible be taken from among the synodal judges.[95] If the Bishop does not assign an auditor for a cause, the Official may select one from among those approved by

[91] Cfr. p. 75 sq.

[92] Can. 193; D'Angelo, *La Curia Diocesana* II, p. 72.

[93] Can. 1582; Schmalzgrueber, *Jus Ecclesiasticum Universum*, Lib. II, Tit. I, n. 15.

[94] Noval, *De Processibus*, n. 71; Roberti, *De Processibus*, n. 112.

[95] Can. 1581, §1.

the Bishop. The power of the auditor is ordinary if he is permanently attached to a tribunal and delegated if he is chosen for a single case by the Ordinary or the judge.[96] Before entering upon his work the auditor will take the oath *de munere fideliter implendo et secreto servando*.[97] Exceptions against him are heard by the Official.[98]

Duties of the Auditor. The duties of the auditor, unless they are outlined in the mandate of his appointment, depend to a great extent on the will of the tribunal. In general it may be said that if the auditor is not at the same time the *ponens* of the collegiate tribunal, all the acts necessary for the construction of a case may be entrusted to him, but he does not pass upon their admission or worth.

While the acceptance or rejection of the *libellus*, the citing of the parties and the *litis contestatio* belong more properly to the duties of the Official or the presiding judge of the tribunal, in ordinary contentious causes they may be entrusted to the auditor. He may cite witnesses,[99] examine them,[100] examine documents,[101] assign the terms for completing proofs and discussions,[102] receive the oaths of the parties,[103] witnesses,[104] experts,[105] the reports of the experts,[106] and conduct the local inspection.[107] Briefly he may execute all the acts, from the acceptance of the libellus to the publication of the process, but none of those acts through which a cause is defined or settled.

In criminal and mixed causes when an investigation precedes the trial,[108] the citation for this is made by the Ordinary, not by the

[96] Roberti, *De Processibus*, n. 110.
[97] Can. 1621, §1.
[98] Can. 1614, §3.
[99] Can. 1582.
[100] Can. 1773.
[101] Can. 1821, §2.
[102] Can. 1862.
[103] Can. 1774.
[104] Can. 1767, §1.
[105] Can. 1797, §1.
[106] Can. 1801, §1.
[107] Can. 1807.
[108] Can. 1939.

Official without a mandate of the Bishop [109] and certainly not by the auditor. It could be inferred from the same canons [110] that the examination of the parties and the *litis contestatio* in any cause are not properly the work of the auditor. In criminal causes when the crime is notorious or entirely certain, and no investigation is required, decision as to the notoriety or certainty of the case is to be given by the Bishop.[111]

An auditor can be removed at any time during a trial for any just cause by the one who has appointed him, but care should be taken that the parties to the trial are placed at no disadvantage or expense through his removal.[112]

Art. III. Nature of the Power of the Diocesan Collegiate Tribunal

Whether the tribunal enjoys ordinary or delegated jurisdiction is a matter of controversy.

Roberti seems to consider this power ordinary because he cannot conceive of the Legislator as wishing to create the anomaly of a tribunal composed in part of the Official or the Bishop who certainly possess ordinary jurisdiction, and for the rest, associate judges with only delegated power.[113] Blat [114] also considers this jurisdiction as ordinary.

Other commentators generally regard the power of synodal judges as delegated and say that while these ecclestiastics habitually bear the title judge they do not actually possess jurisdiction and are not judges unless they are delegated to hear a cause or a class of causes or delegated *ad universitatem causarum.* They cannot judge any cause unless it has been assigned to them by legitimate authority and as soon as sentence is passed in the cause or group of causes which they were delegated to hear by the Bishop, their

109 Can. 1946.

110 Cans. 1939-1946.

111 Can. 1955; Noval, n. 135.

112 Can. 1583.

113 Roberti, *De Processibus,* I, n. 103, p. 173, footnote 4.

114 Blat, *Commentarium,* Lib. IV, p. 45.

jurisdiction ceases. Nevertheless all insist that a tribunal so constituted by the Bishop and composed of the Official and synodal judges *in actu* must be considered an ordinary tribunal.[115] There is no appeal from it to the Ordinary but only to a superior tribunal.

Art. IV. Causes Proper to the Diocesan Collegiate Tribunal

The causes submitted to the Collegiate Tribunal of the diocesan curia may be divided into two classes:

1. Causes reserved by the law itself.
2. Causes which may be referred to the Collegiate Tribunal.

A. *Causes reserved by law to the Collegiate Tribunal.*

Can. 1576. §1. Reprobata contraria consuetudine et revocato quolibet contrario privilegio:

1°. Causae contentiosae de vinculo sacrae ordinationis, et matrimonii, vel de iuribus aut bonis temporalibus cathedralis ecclesiae: itemque criminales in quibus res est de privatione beneficii inamovibilis aut de irroganda vel declaranda excommunicatione, tribunali collegiali trium iudicum reservantur:

2°. Causae vero quibus agitur de delictis quae depositionis, privationis perpetuae habitus ecclesiastici, vel degradationis poenam important, reservantur tribunali quinque iudicum.

1. The following causes are reserved by law to a tribunal of three judges. Cases involving:

a. The bond of sacred orders.[116]

b. The bond of marriage.

[115] Wernz-Vidal, *Jus Canonicum*, IV, n. 90; Cocchi, *Commentarium*, Lib. IV, Part I, Sect. I, Tit. II, n. 19; Vermeersch-Creusen, *Epitome*, III, n. 35; Noval, *De Processibus*, n. 118.

[116] A recent instruction of the Sacred Congregation of the Sacraments has modified this canon and withdrawn causes concerning the bond of Sacred Orders from the competence of the diocesan tribunal. Cfr. Instr. S. C. de Sac., June 9, 1931, A.A.S., XXIII (1931), 457 sq.

c. The rights or goods of the cathedral church.

d. The judicial deprivation of an irremovable benefice.

e. The judicial infliction or declaration of the penalty of excommunication.

2. The following causes are reserved by law to a tribunal of five judges.

Criminal causes so serious in their nature as to involve the penalty of:

a. Deposition.

b. Perpetual privation of the ecclesiastical habit.

c. Degradation.

The prescriptions of Canon 1567, §1, 1° and 2° are absolute and every contrary custom must be regarded as unreasonable. All contrary privileges in regard to these matters are revoked. The provisions of concordats are, however, excepted.[117]

B. *Cases which may be referred to the Collegiate Tribunal*

Canon 1572. §2. Si vero agatur de iuribus aut bonis temporalibus Episcopi aut mensae vel Curiae dioecesanae, controversia dirimenda deferatur vel, Episcopo consentiente, ad dioecesanum tribunal collegiale quod constat officiali et duobus iudicibus synodalibus antiquioribus, vel ad iudicem immediate superiorem.

Whenever the temporal rights or temporal property of the Bishop or of the *mensa epicopalis* or of the diocesan curia are involved in a controversy the Bishop *may* entrust the cause to the hearing and decision of the official and the two senior synodal judges, or he may take the cause to the immediately higher court.

Can. 1576. §2. Loci ordinarius tribunali collegiali trium vel quinque iudicum cognitionem committere potest etiam aliarum causarum, idque praesertim faciat quando de causis agitur quae, attentis temporis, loci et personarum adiunctis et materia iudicii, difficiliores et maioris momenti videantur.

[117] Can. 3.

The second paragraph of Canon 1576 permits the Bishop to entrust to a tribunal of three or five judges other causes besides those mentioned in Can. 1576, §1, 1° and 2°, which are more difficult and important by reason of circumstances of time, place and persons or the matter involved.

CHAPTER III

GENERAL REGULATIONS TO BE OBSERVED BY THE DIOCESAN COLLEGIATE TRIBUNAL

WITH the organization of the diocesan collegiate tribunal effected, and provision having been made for the proper personnel, attention is now directed to the general rules governing the manner in which this tribunal shall function.

ART. I. JURIDICAL QUALIFICATIONS

Besides those mental and moral qualifications spoken of in a previous chapter which every judge must possess, before the tribunal can admit or summon a person to trial, it must be sure of two things; first, whether it is competent; [1] and secondly, whether the person who seeks its services has a right to stand in court,[2] either personally [3] or through others.[4] To pass a valid sentence the tribunal must have jurisdiction over the persons and the matter in question unless jurisdiction is supplied as in common error.[5] This incompetency of the tribunal may be absolute [6] or relative.[7] If the tribunal is competent, and the person has a right to the ministry of the tribunal, the tribunal is obliged to grant all applicants the ministry of their office,[8] or they can be forced to do so by ecclesiastical penalties.[9] To incur these penalties the tribunal must be certainly and evidently competent, for if it is not competent or only doubtfully competent it is not so held. The party must legitimately

[1] Can. 1609, §1.
[2] Can. 1609, §2.
[3] Cans. 1646-1654.
[4] Cans. 1655-1666.
[5] Can. 209.
[6] Cans. 1556-1557.
[7] Cans. 1558-1568.
[8] Can. 1608.
[9] Can. 1625, §1.

seek the services of the tribunal, that is he must seek a declaration on a juridical fact on which the Church has the right to judge, and which is not notorious or evident but truly doubtful; that it concern the petitioner, and entail the prosecution or vindication of physical or moral persons, or a declaration of juridical facts concerning such persons in the case of contentious suits, or the infliction or declaration of penalties in criminal suits; [10] and that the party is not evidently deprived of the right to this judicial action in general, and to those things in particular about which he seeks a solution.[11]

It is not necessary that this investigation be entered in the acts of the case.[12]

A. *Exceptions to the Competency of the Collegiate Tribunal.* A tribunal decides its own competency whether it is an ordinary or a delegated tribunal.

Exceptions may be taken to the competency of the tribunal. In questions of relative incompetency the tribunal itself decides generally through the Official,[13] and from this decision in favor of the competency of the tribunal there is no appeal.[14]

If the tribunal declares itself incompetent the party who regards himself as injured may within ten days take an appeal to the higher court.[15]

If the tribunal finds itself absolutely incompetent it must declare this incompetency at any stage of the trial, and in whatever instance the case may be in if it has been appealed,[16] or if no appeal is made the trial should be declared null. The tribunal is bound *ex officio* to do this even if no exception is taken by the parties. Relative incompetency should be declared and exceptions taken before the close of the *litis contestatio*,[17] when a case becomes proper to the court where the action was begun.

If there arises a conflict between two tribunals as to which of

[10] Can. 1552, §1, §2.
[11] Can. 1609, §2.
[12] Can. 1609, §3.
[13] Can. 1610, §1.
[14] Can. 1610, §2.
[15] Can. 1610, §3.
[16] Can. 1611.
[17] Can. 1725, §1, n. 2.

them is competent in some affair, the matter should be settled by the immediately higher tribunal; and if they are subject to different higher tribunals the question is settled by the higher tribunal of that court to which the case was first taken; if the tribunal has no court of appeal, the dispute is settled by the Legate of the Holy See or by the Signatura Apostolica.[18]

B. *Other Exceptions.* Every judge of the tribunal must be above suspicion. There is good reason to suspect that a judge acting in certain cases will be naturally inclined to favor one side. The Code forbids a judge to act in the case of a person related to him by reason of consanguinity and affinity in any degree of the direct line or in the first or second degree of the collateral line; or to whom he has been at any time a guardian or trustee; or in the case of an enemy or of an intimate friend; or in any case in which he has much to gain or lose, or in which he has been an advocate or procurator at any time.[19] Exception on these same points may be taken against the defender of the bond or any other officer of the court.[20]

C. *By whom are these exceptions heard?* If an exception on any of these grounds is taken against the Bishop, acting as head of the tribunal, ruling on the question of suspicion should be made by the immediately higher judge.[21]

Exceptions against the Official are heard by the Bishop.[22] If exceptions are proposed against any other judge they are decided by the Official. If exception is taken against the majority of the judges of the tribunal or against the tribunal as a whole when presided over by the Official, the exception is heard by the Bishop. If the exception is taken against the whole or a majority of a delegated diocesan tribunal, the Bishop decides the question; if against a single member of the delegated tribunal the question is decided by the other members.[23] Exceptions against any officer of the tribunal

[18] Can. 1612.

[19] Can. 1613, §1. Cfr. Noval, *De Processibus,* n. 196.

[20] Can. 1613.

[21] Cans. 1614, §2, 1594.

[22] Can. 1614, §1.

[23] Can. 1614, §1.

are heard by the Official or in the case of a delegated tribunal by the presiding judge.[24]

If exceptions are upheld the case stays in the same instance but the officers are changed. The Ordinary appoints other judges or officers in the place of those suspected. If the exception was made against the Ordinary himself the immediately higher judge appoints other judges to try the case.

When such an exception is taken, the principal process must be stopped until the incidental question is decided. The acts in which the suspected judge participated are null.[25] They may be healed by consent of the parties concerned. If they will not consent to this, the acts should be done over, or a sanatio asked from legitimate authority.

These exceptions can be proposed by the parties to a suit and by their procurators, by the defender of the bond and the promoter of justice, but unless they are proposed before the sentence they do not nullify the acts of the process.[26] Ordinarily a judge or an officer of the tribunal finding himself in these circumstances should withdraw from the case, but if he does not do so the sentence is not invalid. The manner and time during which this exception should be proposed shall be treated in a later article.[27]

Art. II. The Integrity of Judges and Other Ministers of a Tribunal

An ecclesiastical judge as well as others who assist in ecclesiastical courts must be above suspicion in every way. They must not only abstain from acting in cases in which their own advantage or the advantage of their friends might appear to conflict with the duty of strict impartiality (as when they have personal litigation in court, or when a near relative is party in a controversy, or when one of the contestants is their personal, fraternal, or political friend or enemy, etc.,[28]) but they must likewise abstain from accepting all

[24] Can. 1614, §3.

[25] De Luca, *De Judiciis*, disp., III, n. 7.

[26] Roberti, *De Processibus*, n. 156.

[27] Cfr. Chapter IV, Art. V.

[28] Can. 1613.

gifts that are offered in connection with or in reference to a trial, even after the trial has ended.[29] There is not question here of the salary which a judge may receive from funds set aside for this purpose, or of legitimate fees set up in a province for judicial acts. Neither is it necessary to suppose that the legislator had in mind only bribes used to influence a judge either to decide in one's favor or to hear one case before another, or to hasten a case or to decide for one side when the evidence is equal. All goods of whatever nature given as free gifts with no condition attached are to be understood. The reception of any gift is bound to result in mistrust and scandal and is consequently forbidden. Some authors, principally Noval [30] and Augustine [31] go so far as to say that food and drink such as are usually offered to a visitor are forbidden by this canon. While the acceptance of such marks of civility or hospitality does not seem unlawful in itself, even these should be avoided when there is a possibility of scandal or suspicion.

Art. III. The Oath Taken by Judges, Officers of the Tribunal, and Others in Court; Obligation of Secrecy

A. *The Oath.* With the exception of the Bishop when he sits in person in the tribunal, all persons who constitute or assist the diocesan collegiate tribunal must take an oath that they will fulfill their office properly and faithfully.[32] Hence the Official, Vice-official, Synodal and Pro-synodal Judges, Auditors, the Promoter of Justice, the Defender of the Bond, the Notaries, Messengers, Constables and Interpreters must take the oath.

This oath is taken at the beginning of their office if they are regular officers of the tribunal or before the beginning of the trial if they are appointed only for a particular case.[33] This oath is taken before the Ordinary or his delegate, or before the Official or his delegate if he appoints any of these officers.[34]

[29] Can. 1624.

[30] Noval, *De Processibus,* n. 215.

[31] Augustine, *A Commentary on Canon Law,* VII, n. 71.

[32] Can. 1621, §1.

[33] Can. 1621, §2.

[34] Can. 1621, §3.

This oath, like all oaths used in a judicial process, must be taken personally by those upon whom the oath is incumbent. A notary should witness the oath and make a record of it, which record is to be preserved in the archives.[35] Note must also be made of this in the minutes of the trial. Accompanying the appointment of every such officer, if he is permanently attached to a tribunal, should be a notice suggesting to him that he appear before the Ordinary or his delegate and the notary at a specified time to take the oath. In regard to the manner of taking this oath the Code requires that judges and other officers of the tribunal first invoke the name of God, priests touch their breast and laymen touch the Book of the Gospels, and recite the approved formula. The obligations arising from this oath of office taken by judges and other officers of the tribunal are as wide as the duties involved, and if through neglect or malice they are efficaciously and subjectively the cause of serious harm to a litigant through an act that is objectively unjust, they not only commit grievous sin but are likewise morally responsible for the damage done.

Whenever the oath is taken during a trial by the parties, witnesses, or experts it must always be taken in the presence of the Official or his delegate, and the notary, and the latter must make a record of it. The formula must always be approved by the Official or the presiding judge.[36] Before administering the oath to litigants, witnesses and experts, the one who administers the oath must always remind them of the sacredness of the act, and of the seriousness of the crime of perjury, and of the ecclesiastical penalties to which one becomes liable who, after taking the oath, tells a falsehood in court.[37] Besides this oath to speak the truth which parties, witnesses and experts must take, the parties may be called upon to take the supplementary oath, in certain cases in order to supply missing proofs,[38] the estimatory oath, which may be demanded to ascertain the amount of damage due the injured party after the right to

[35] Can. 1621, §3.
[36] Can. 1622, §3.
[37] Can. 1622, §2.
[38] Cans. 1829-1831.

indemnity has been established,[39] and the decisive oath, which under certain conditions may be used by the parties before the trial begins, or may be demanded by one party of the other during the trial.[40]

B. *The Obligation of Secrecy.* The obligation of secrecy about judicial acts may be regarded under a two-fold aspect—1. the obligation of secrecy incumbent on judges and other ministers of the tribunal, which is the secret of office; 2. the obligation of secrecy which may be imposed on others who take part in a trial.

The secret of office binds judges and other ministers of the tribunal in regard to the votes, opinions and discussions advanced in the meetings which are held preliminary to the final sentence whether the discussions concern interlocutory sentences or the definitive sentence. Strict secrecy must be observed perpetually in regard to all ballots, views and discussions of these meetings. *Per se* they can be revealed to no one.[41]

In criminal causes all knowledge acquired by virtue of their office must be kept secret as long as the trial lasts, but once sentence is passed those matters which are revealed in connection with the sentence need not be kept longer, unless the tribunal imposes a special precept to this effect. Whatever is not revealed in the sentence should be kept secret always.

In contentious causes judges and officers must keep judicial knowledge secret as long and whenever the revelation of that knowledge would be detrimental or prejudicial to the parties.[42]

Secrecy may be imposed on the parties, witnesses, experts, advocates and procurators if the nature of the case or the evidence presented is such that from the divulging of the proceedings and proofs the good reputation of others might be endangered or discord, scandal or other untoward consequences might result.[43]

[39] Cans. 1832-1833.

[40] Cans. 1834-1836.

[41] Cans. 1623, §1; 1871, §2.

[42] Cfr. Wernz-Vidal, *Jus Canonicum,* VI, n. 155.

[43] Can. 1623.

Art. IV. Sanctions and Penalties for Judges and Other Ministers of the Tribunal

To safeguard the administration of justice, the Church not only requires judges and other ministers of the tribunal to take an oath to fulfill properly and faithfully the duties of their office but also attaches severe penalties to transgressions against the duties of their office.

The following crimes enumerated in Canon 1625 must be regarded as violations of the oath of office, and are punishable in the several ways outlined in this canon. Judges could violate the duties of their office in the following ways: 1. when certainly and evidently competent and when no exception has been taken against them they refuse their ministry to those who have a right to it; 2. when without a juridical reason they declare themselves competent in any case, e.g., where their incompetency is absolute; 3. when they maliciously and with culpable negligence follow an invalid procedure and render an act null, that is when they deliberately and knowingly omit any of the essential requisites or formalities which the Sacred Canons require in the process, e.g., the requisites for a sentence outlined in Canons 1892, 1894;[44] 4. when they act unjustly against a litigant, for instance, by inflicting a censure on an innocent party, accepting bribes for favoring a litigant; 5. when they in any other way act against their conscience and thereby injure a litigant. Judges guilty of any one of these crimes may be punished by the Ordinary with penalties proportionate to their guilt, to the harm done, or to the scandal caused and may even be deprived of their office.[45] If the Ordinary himself is guilty of any of these crimes he can be punished by the Apostolic See. The imputability of such crimes will depend on the will of the delinquent (dolus) and on the extent to which his ignorance of the law, or his omission of proper diligence was culpable.[46] A judge is morally obliged to repair the injury done as far as possible and to

[44] Can. 1680.

[45] Can. 1625, §1.

[46] Can. 2199.

indemnify the injured party for any expenses incurred in consequence of his wrongdoing.

Judges who violate the secrecy of their office,[47] or who communicate the secret proceedings spoken of in Canon 1623, §2, §3, as explained in a previous article may be punished with a fine and other proportionate penalties, including deprivation of office and even with more severe penalties if particular regulations of the tribunal provide graver penalties. Of course the revelation must be intentional. Penalties for the violation of the secret may be inflicted by the Ordinary, or if the Ordinary is guilty by the Apostolic See.[48] Other ministers of the tribunal, such as the notary, the defender of the bond, the promoter of justice, auditors, etc., may be punished in the same way for similar offenses and the penalties may be inflicted by the Official.[49] The Official likewise has coercive power over disobedient litigants, witnesses, and experts. He can force them to testify and to fulfill their duties and can inflict proportionate penalties.[50] The penalties may be inflicted on the demand of the parties or *ex-officio*.

ART. V. THE ORDER OF PROCEDURE

The tribunal is ordinarily obliged to hear cases in the order in which they were submitted to it.[51] A case is legally submitted through the filing of the *libellus* or bill of complaint. If the tribunal having considered a case objectively thinks that it should be advanced, this may be done by a decree of the Official.[52] From this decree there is no appeal.[53]

The legislator wishes trials to proceed in an orderly fashion, hence the Code requires that certain pleas be made at specified stages of the trial under the penalty of forfeiting the right to make them. Certain exceptions must be proposed and solved, before the

[47] Can. 1623, §1, §2.
[48] Can. 1652, §2.
[49] Can. 1625, §3.
[50] Cans. 1705, 1640, §2.
[51] Can. 1627, §1.
[52] Can. 1627, §2.
[53] Can. 1880, §6.

joining of issues (*litis contestatio*), which establishes the instance. Such are dilatory exceptions of suspicion,[54] exceptions against the manner of the trial.[55] They can be made later only if they emerge after the contestation or the party raising them affirms under oath that he did not have knowledge of them before.[56] But exceptions to the absolute incompetency of a judge and the exception of excommunication against a plaintiff or a judge can be made at any time of a trial.[57]

Peremptory exceptions which put an end to a trial, e.g., the exception of *res judicata*,[58] agreement,[59] etc., must also be made before the joining of issues (*litis contestatio*); if made later and the plea is rejected, the party making them is liable for the cost unless he can prove he did not maliciously delay raising the exceptions.[60] Other peremptory exceptions may be tried after the *litis contestatio*.[61] Counter claims (*reconventiones*) should be made immediately after the *litis contestatio*, but they may be brought later. They must, however, be heard before the final sentence.[62] Questions of security, expenses, gratuitous defense, etc., should be settled before the *litis contestatio*.[63]

Exceptions against witnesses must be made within three days after the names of the witnesses have been proposed to the other party.[64] Exceptions against testimony, the manner in which it is taken, etc., are usually made after the publication of the testimony.

Prejudicial questions arising after the principal question has been submitted to the tribunal should be settled before the principal question.[65]

[54] Can. 1614.
[55] Cans. 1708-1715.
[56] Can. 1628, §1.
[57] Can. 1628, §2, §3.
[58] Can. 1902.
[59] Cans. 1926-1927.
[60] Can. 1629, §1.
[61] Can. 1629, §2.
[62] Can. 1630, §1.
[63] Can. 1631.
[64] Can. 1764, §4.
[65] Can. 1632.

Incidental questions should be settled in such a way that the solution of one prepares the way for the solution of others. If there is no logical connection between several incidental questions the one first proposed should be solved first, actions *de spolio*[66] excepted.

Art. VI. Delays

Trials should be terminated within a reasonable length of time but delays are sometimes necessary so the Code permits a judge to grant and prolong them under certain conditions.

The *fatalia legis* or the fixed periods which are granted by law for the execution of certain judicial acts cannot be prolonged.[67] Such are the ten days allowed for appeal against a judge who declares himself relatively incompetent,[68] the one year for action for injury, etc. There are other delays as *termini judiciales* which may be granted by the judge for a just cause and the *termini conventionales* which the law permits the parties to fix by mutual agreement. These may be prolonged at the request of the parties or by the judge *ex officio,* after he has heard those concerned. Judges are cautioned to watch that a trial is not protracted by prorogation.[69] Prorogation is always understood to extend to the next following day that is not a holiday if a term set by a judge for a judicial action falls on a holiday and provided no mention is made in the decree that the tribunal does not sit on that day.[70]

The Code furnishes a legal remedy against delays in abatement of the instance which provides that if no lawful impediment can be alleged and no procedural act has been done in a court of first instance for two years or in a court of appeal for one year, the suit is automatically dropped.[71] The acts of the case remain effective for another instance.

[66] Cans. 1633, 1698-1699.
[67] Can. 1634, §1.
[68] Can. 1610.
[69] Can. 1634, §3.
[70] Can. 1634.
[71] Cans. 1736-1739.

Art. VII. Place and Time of Sessions

An ecclesiastical judge or tribunal cannot exercise jurisdiction outside the limits of his own territory, unless he is forcibly expelled from his own territory or is prevented from exercising jurisdiction there, when he may exercise judicial jurisdiction anywhere but he should inform the local Ordinary of the fact.[72] The Code directs bishops to designate a judgment hall in the episcopal city as the ordinary place for trials. The Ordinary may set up a tribunal anywhere in his territory provided that place be not exempt. In this hall the Crucifix should occupy a conspicuous place and a Book of the Gospels must be provided, also chairs and tables. Provision should likewise be made for waiting rooms for witnesses, files and other necessary equipment.

Convenient days and hours should be established by decree of the Ordinary in every diocese during which regular access can be had to the court, i.e., the Official and a notary to request their services in the administration of justice.[73] However, for a just reason the faithful may invoke the services of the court at any time to protect their rights or the common good.[74]

All Sundays and holydays of obligation and the last three days of Holy Week are considered as holidays (*dies feriati*), and on these days it is forbidden to issue summons, have court hearings, examine parties, witnesses or experts, accept proofs or issue or execute decrees and sentences except in cases of necessity, or when Christian charity or the public welfare demand an exception. An example would be if witnesses could not appear conveniently on another day. Everyone interested in the matter should be notified. The Official shall determine in each individual case what acts may be performed on holidays or what acts performed on those days are valid or invalid.

Art. VIII. Persons Admitted to Trials

Only those persons who are necessary for conducting a trial are to be admitted to the court sessions. All others are to be

[72] Can. 1636.
[73] Can. 1638, §1.
[74] Can. 1638, §2.

excluded. Hence, during the examination of the parties beside the judges and the notary, the advocates or procurators of both parties and if the character of the case requires it, the defender of the bond and the promoter of justice and interpreters may be present.[75] During the examination of the witnesses all except the judges of the tribunal and the notary and the procurators and advocates of both parties are to be excluded. This exclusion extends both to parties and to witnesses unless at the discretion of the tribunal confrontation of parties with witnesses or witnesses with other witnesses is permitted. It is understood that collusion on the part of advocates and procurators is forbidden.[76] Parties, their procurators and advocates are regularly present when experts report to the tribunal. If the sentence is published by citing the parties to hear it read in court, ordinarily only the parties themselves and their advocates and procurators, the judges and the notary are present although the promoter of justice and the defender of the bond may be present. The judges can bind by an oath to secrecy, witnesses, experts, litigants, their lawyers and proxies, if the nature of the case or if the evidence is such that from the divulging of the proceedings and proofs the good reputation of others might be endangered or discord, scandal or other untoward consequences might result.[77]

Respect and obedience to the court must be shown at all times, and persons failing in this may be summarily forced to obey through censures and other proportionate penalties, to be inflicted by presiding judge of the tribunal in whose presence they misbehave.[78] Advocates and procurators failing in the respect and reverence due the court may be deprived by the court of the right to appear before it.

Art. IX. Expenses of a Trial: Gratuitous Services

The costs of a trial usually are paid by the litigants unless due to circumstances the parties are released from this burden. The

[75] Cans. 1745, §2; 1773, §1.

[76] Can. 1771.

[77] Can. 1623.

[78] Can. 1640, §2.

tribunal may and usually does in contentious cases demand that a certain sum be deposited by the parties with the court or Chancery to guarantee the expenses of a trial.[79]

Fixed amounts or a definite schedule of costs to be paid by the parties should be fixed by the Bishops of every province during the provincial council. This schedule should prescribe the charges for the general expenses of the court, for the fees of advocates and procurators, for translations and copies of documents, for the verification of documents, and for the copying certificates or documents from the archives.[80]

The expenses which must be borne by the litigants are the costs of the operation of the court itself, that is the expenses of the notary, the judges, auditors of the tribunal in sending notices, citations, copies of testimony, taking testimony, etc., excluding always of course, the salaries of the judges and other officers which are paid by the diocese.

Witness fees and the fees of experts, compensation for loss of time, traveling expenses, etc., incurred while attending the trial are paid by litigants in the amount determined by the court.

Usually the plaintiff must guarantee the costs for acts which the tribunal has to perform *ex officio*. The party who requests that witnesses or experts be summoned must pay the costs.[81]

At the close of the trial the party who loses the suit must as a rule stand the cost of the entire trial and refund to the victor the expenses incurred by him during the trial. However, if the litigants are related, or if the victory of either side is only partial, or if the case dealt with a very difficult question, or for any other reasonable cause the costs may be prorated between the parties.[82] If either the plaintiff or the defendant commences or prosecutes a trial without the semblance of justice, that is rashly, the guilty party may be condemned to pay the costs of the trial and likewise to indemnify the other party for any loss sustained.[83] The final sentence should

[79] Can. 1908.
[80] Can. 1909, §1.
[81] Can. 1909, §2.
[82] Can. 1911.
[83] Can. 1910.

always contain the decision of the tribunal concerning the expenses of the trial, naming the party who is to pay them or prorating the costs between the parties.[84] If several persons are interested in a cause in which the obligation is joint and several, the tribunal should condemn each for the whole (*in solidum*) otherwise it shall condemn them to pay each his share.[85] If a litigant believes himself aggrieved by the ruling of the court on expenditures he may within ten days raise an objection before the same tribunal and it may either change or modify the cost imposed. A separate appeal on the costs of a trial cannot be made, but an appeal against the principal issue always implies an appeal from the ruling of the costs of a trial,[86] and the appeal court may at its discretion modify the tax of the first court. Since the decision of an ecclesiastical court binds in conscience, the costs of a trial when assessed must be considered as an obligation binding in conscience.

Poor people who are unable to pay the costs of a trial are entitled to the services of the court gratuitously. Those who seek total or partial exemption from the costs of a trial must petition the court for exemption. The petition shall contain an exact account of their financial standing, and this statement should be endorsed by trustworthy persons known to the court like the pastor of the party whom the court may question about their financial standing. This petition should likewise contain proof that the party did not engage in futile or rash litigation.[87] The judge before he admits or rejects this petition should investigate the financial standing of the petitioner and give a hearing to the promoter of justice on the question. This exemption may be revoked at any time if the assertions of the petitioner about poverty are found not to be true.[88]

The Code does not define the term *pauperes* but leaves it to the discretion of the court to decide whether a person is entitled to an entire or only a partial remission of the cost of the trial. The court

[84] Can. 1873, §1, n. 4.
[85] Can. 1912.
[86] Can. 1910.
[87] Can. 1915, §1.
[88] Can. 1915.

should take into consideration the circumstances of wages, dependents, etc.

The poor are likewise entitled to the free services of an advocate. In each case the court shall assign an advocate from among those approved by the Bishop [89] or if there are no approved advocates the judge should ask the local Ordinary to appoint a qualified person to represent the poor person.[90] This advocate cannot without a reasonable cause approved by the judge, refuse his services. If he refuses he may be punished with an appropriate penalty even with privation of his office of advocate.[91]

Art. X. Records

Quod non est in actis non est in mundo is a fundamental principle of ecclesiastical courts. All the acts of a trial are committed to writing.[92] The record of a trial contains the *acta causac* and the *acta processus.*

The *acta causae* are those which relate to the merits of the case; the *acta processus* relate to the form of the procedure. To the *acta causae* belong the bill of complaint and the answer of the defendent, all decrees defining incidental questions, which touch on the merits of the case, proofs of every kind, the defense, and all sentences either interlocutory or definitive.

The *acta processus* are citations of parties, witnesses, experts, defender of the bond, promoter of justice, decrees that pertain to the form of the process, the minutes of the process, notifications, etc.

The records should as far as possible be written in Latin. However, citations, the oaths of the parties and witnesses, the questions and answers of the parties, witnesses, the relations and oaths of experts may be drawn up in the vernacular.[93] Every case when received should receive a number and this number should appear on all documents pertaining to the case thereafter. Each page of the record must be numbered and bear the seal of the court and the

[89] Can. 1916, §1.
[90] Can. 1916, §2.
[91] Can. 1916, §1.
[92] Can. 1642, §1.
[93] Can. 1642, §2.

signature of the notary.[94] The Official and the notary must sign every proceeding when it is completed, interrupted or adjourned.[95] Whenever the signature of the parties or witnesses is required and the party or witness is unable or refuses to sign his name, a note to that effect shall be made in the acts and the Official or his delegate and the notary shall attest that the act itself was read verbatim to the party or to the witness and that the party or the witness could not or did not want to subscribe to it.[96] Durable paper and special ink should be used in the making of the acts.

Files. The files of the court should be organized with a view to efficiency and economy of effort. Such modern devices as flat filing, card indexing, etc., may be used to advantage. There should be secret and public archives.

Cases that are finished and pending might well be placed in separate files. Cases when finished should be bound in a fascicle with an index of all acts and documents. It may be found convenient to inclose cases pending in covers, upon the back of which the progress and present disposition of the case is currently recorded, so that this information is available at a glance to the directing authority of the court.

Copies of the record of a case which are sent to a court of appeal should be bound and indexed and should always be accompanied by an affidavit of the notary affirming that the copies are exact and complete, or if the original acts are sent they likewise must be certified by the notary. When copies of the acts are sent to a court where the vernacular is unknown the acts should be translated into Latin and the faithfulness of the translation guaranteed. Acts that are not composed in the proper form and style may be refused by the higher judge and the notary through whose negligence this has happened is bound to have them redrafted and forwarded at his own expense.[97]

At the completion of a trial such documents as testimonials, deeds, certificates, etc., which are required by the court should be

[94] Can. 1643, §1.

[95] Can. 1643, §2.

[96] Can. 1643, §3.

[97] Can. 1644.

restored to their owners. But other documents should be deposited in the diocesan archives either public or secret as the nature of the document demands. Copies of judicial acts acquired in a trial are not allowed to be given out without an order from the Official.[98]

[98] Can. 1645.

CHAPTER IV

PARTICULAR DUTIES OF THE INDIVIDUAL JUDGES OF THE TRIBUNAL AND OF THE TRIBUNAL AS A WHOLE

ATTENTION is now directed to the internal organization of the tribunal. Concretely the question presented in the articles of this chapter is the role that each member of the tribunal plays in the adjudication of cases presented to it for consideration. Who presides over the tribunal? What acts may the presiding judge execute alone? Who is the *ponens* and what are his duties? What acts must be done by the integral college? These questions suggest the topics for the succeeding articles. Here no attempt is made to consider other than the basic principles which determine the general character of the system employed.

ART. I. THE PRESIDING JUDGE

Can. 1577. §2. Eidem praeest officialis vel vice-officialis, cuius est processum dirigere, et decernere quae pro iustitiae administratione in causa quae agitur necessaria sunt.

Can. 1578. Exceptis causis de quibus in can. 1572, §2, Episcopus semper potest tribunali ipse per se praeesse; sed valde expedit ut causas, praesertim criminales et contentiosas gravis momenti, iudicandas relinquat tribunali ordinario, cui praesit officialis vel vice-officialis.

While the Bishop may preside over the collegiate tribunal except in those causes mentioned in Canon 1572, §2, ordinarily the Official presides over the tribunal, directs the procedure, and decides what is necessary for the administration of justice in a given case.[1]

[1] Can. 1577, §2.

The power of the presiding judge depends in many things on the practice of the tribunal and the will of the college. Some acts can be entrusted to him singly, and are by local custom, which in other tribunals may be done by the integral college. The Code directs the collegiate tribunal to proceed collegiately, and requires absolutely the intervention of all the judges of the tribunal in the rendition of the final sentence for the validity of the sentence.[2] Since auditors are generally given a wide range of power by the tribunal the necessity for all members of the tribunal to be present, excepting at the final sentence, would be rare.[3]

The presiding judge may accept or reject the *libellus*[4] in the less difficult cases, but in the more difficult cases this should be done by the integral college. He hears exceptions against the promoter of justice, the defender of the bond and other auxiliary officers of the tribunal. He appoints the *ponens*. He may preside at the *litis contestatio*.[5] He fixes an appropriate interval of time within which the parties must procure and complete proofs of their case. He may prolong this interval at the request of the parties but he should see that the trial is not unduly protracted. He proposes the questions submitted by the parties, their advocates, the defender of the bond, the promoter of justice and the other judges to the parties, witnesses and experts.

The Bishop may give the Official general delegation to select the turns of synodal judges.[6] He may summon the parties and witnesses.[7] He may exclude unfit and suspected witnesses. When witnesses are disobedient, refuse to appear or stay away without a legitimate excuse, they may be punished by the presiding judge with congruous penalties in proportion to the damage resulting to the parties.[8] When witnesses because of circumstances such as sickness, distance, or age, are unable to appear later in the trial, the

[2] Cans. 1577, §1, n. 1; 1871, §1; 1874, §5; 1892, §1.

[3] Noval, *De Processibus*, n. 126; Roberti, *De Processibus*, I, p. 173.

[4] Cans. 1709-1710.

[5] Can. 1727.

[6] *Apollinaris* IV (1931), 303.

[7] Can. 1712, §1.

[8] Can. 1766.

presiding judge may permit their depositions to be taken even before the *litis contestatio.*[9] He may choose the experts necessary in certain cases.[10] He fixes the expense allowance of witnesses and the fees of experts.[11] When in the course of a trial, doubt is raised as to the authenticity of certain documents he may order the originals exhibited and examined in the presence of the parties on the points in question.[12] He may decide by an interlocutory sentence whether and how the exhibition of certain documents is to be made.[13] He accepts or rejects petitions for exemption or reduction of judicial expenses. He may revoke this exemption or reduction if he finds the declarations of the petitioner about poverty are untrue.[14]

When any single act of the trial is completed, or interrupted and postponed until another session, he signs the document with the notary. He shall prudently prevent too extensive a defense unless this matter is regulated by special laws of the tribunal.[15] He may order the chief documents of the defense or a summary of the acts and documents of the trial printed.[16] He must approve the printing of any act of the case. He appoints the day and the hour at which the members of the tribunal meet to discuss the cause. He is moderator of the discussion which takes place at the meeting of the tribunal when each judge presents his conclusions on the case and they determine the wording of the decisive part of the sentence.[17] He signs all decrees and sentences of the tribunal with the notary. The other judges while subservient to the presiding judge in regard to the discipline of the tribunal enjoy complete liberty of judgment in voting and deciding the sentence of the tribunal.

[9] Can. 1730.
[10] Can. 1793, §1.
[11] Can. 1805.
[12] Can. 1821.
[13] Can. 1824.
[14] Can. 1915.
[15] Can. 1864.
[16] Can. 1863, §3.
[17] Can. 1871, §3, n. 1.

Art. II. The Delegated Judge

A member of the tribunal other than the presiding judge and the *ponens* is sometimes delegated by the tribunal to perform certain acts connected with the cause and thus the necessity of convoking the entire tribunal is avoided. His work may consist in effecting the *litis contestatio,* in the examination of witnesses, receiving the oaths of the parties, conducting local inspection. When the work of the auditor is incomplete or unsatisfactory then this judge may complete the act or acts that are faulty. His power will depend entirely on the will of the college.

Art. III. The Ponens

> **Can. 1584. Tribunalis collegialis praeses debet unum de iudicibus collegii ponentem seu relatorem designare qui in coetu iudicum de causa referat et sententias in scriptis redigat; et ipsi idem praeses potest alium ex iusta causa substituere.**

Canon 1584 prescribes that the Official shortly after the introduction of a cause should appoint as *ponens,* one of the judges of *turnus, per se* distinct from the presiding judge, and the auditor. His duty is to report to the tribunal on the progress of the case and to commit the sentence to writing. This officer known in Canon 1584 as the *ponens* is referred to in Canon 1873, §2, as the *extensor.* This appointment is not absolutely necessary if the presiding judge does the work of the *ponens.* But when one considers the many duties which ordinarily devolve on the Official as presiding judge of the tribunal and as judge sole in the average curia, the utility and relative necessity of this appointment in most cases is quite evident. It is almost impossible for the Official to devote to every case coming before the tribunal that special care and diligent study which each case merits. With the appointment of the *ponens* in every case it is his duty to watch its progress, to urge the completion of the proofs, and at the earliest possible moment to present the results of his study and observation to the other judges in a meeting which should precede the final meeting which is held to discuss the case before the definitive sentence is formulated and published. At this previous meeting he will recall to the judges the various parts of evidence presented, and the different witnesses who testified. He can suggest any inconsistencies and improbabilities he has observed. He can caution the judges about such evidence as is likely to appear entitled to too much or too little weight, about evidence that is inherently weak or strong. In general he will undertake to present to the other judges a full discriminating and well balanced yet brief summary and analysis of the case. There can hardly be any doubt about the immense value of such a summary to the other judges in aiding them to formulate that written opinion which each must bring to the final meeting where the final sentence is drafted.

In the final meeting where the definitive sentence is drafted, the *ponens* will read his opinion first, and he shall be followed by the Official and the other judges in the order of precedence. The *ponens* will then draft the sentence of the tribunal making use of those reasons of fact and of law advanced by the majority of judges or those which the majority decides should be included as motives for the sentence. Attention is called to the fact that the *ponens* unlike the auditor has a decisive vote on the sentence.[18]

Art. IV. The Judicial Functions of the Integral College

Can. 1577. Tribunal collegiale collegialiter procedere debet. . . .

In the evolution of a trial one can distinguish between the work done by the tribunal in determining and investigating facts and that done in interpreting and applying the law to these facts. Frequently the work of determining and investigating facts is entrusted to the auditor, the presiding judge or to a delegated judge. When the trial opens, the parties and witnesses can be brought at once to the point in controversy with no waste of time over formal preliminaries. The necessity for examination of the parties and witnesses before the integral tribunal is greatly reduced and sometimes omitted. The

[18] Can. 1584.

formal introduction of evidence is supplied for by complete typewritten sets of testimony taken by the auditor with the notary, and reports on documents previously inspected. All this is in the hands of the judges, and they are able to proceed with the application of the law to the facts ascertained. The ground is cleared and the judges are at once able to proceed with the study of the case in view of a sentence and to prepare their opinion.

Provided the other prescriptions of the Code are fulfilled such as the presence of the notary, etc., canonists agree that acts of the ordinary diocesan collegiate tribunal other than the sentence are not to be considered invalid if all the judges were not present. Acts which have a direct bearing on the definitive sentence should be heard by the integral college. Such for example would be an incidental question which is so intimately connected with the point at issue, that a decision on it would forestall or amount to the final sentence. All the judges should be present at the sessions in which the decision of the tribunal reached.[19] All the acts whether conducted by the auditor or the presiding judge or delegated judge should be submitted to each member of the tribunal before sentence is passed.

Despite all this, the canon quoted in the beginning of this article is not merely declaratory of the power of the integral tribunal but the legislator wishes this precept requiring the college to proceed collegiately to be carried out whenever possible even in those acts which precede the sentence. The report of the auditor can reproduce only the cold words of the witnesses, while the story that is told in the eyes, the tone of voice and manner of the witness is lost to all but the one who examines the witness. Of gravest importance are such facts as the tone of voice in which a statement is made, the hesitation or readiness with which an answer is given, the zeal with which damaging testimony is given, the looks, shrugs and gestures accompanying it, display of surprise, furtive or meaning glances, self-possession or embarrassment, air of candor or seeming levity, etc., all these circumstances are manifest only to those who actually see and hear the witness.

[19] Noval, *De Processibus*, n. 126; Roberti, *De Processibus*, I, p. 230.

The tribunal then, whenever possible, should proceed collegiately in all the acts of the trial. They should examine the right of the plaintiff to sue, hear exceptions against the presiding judge or any other member of the tribunal, settle incidental questions, be present at the examination of the parties, pass on the admission or exclusion of witnesses, hear them,[20] define the duties of experts, hear and pass on their reports,[21] examine the defense [22] and pass sentence.[23]

If during the course of any of these acts an individual judge wishes to suggest a question or to have a witness called or to have some point clarified he has the right to ask the presiding judge to do what he requests.

The names of the three judges appear on, and they sign the definitive sentence under penalty of nullity.

20 Cans. 1743, §2; 1753, 1758, 1759, 1786, 1789, 1804, 1818, 1828.

21 Cans. 1799, 1800, §2; 1803.

22 Can. 1862.

23 Can. 1871 sqq.

CHAPTER V

THE SENTENCE OF THE COLLEGIATE TRIBUNAL

Before proceeding to question of how the several judges of the tribunal determine the final sentence, it might be well to give some consideration to the manner in which the individual judge should reach his opinion, and the rules which should guide him in formulating his opinion.

Art. I. Rules Which Should Guide the Individual Judge in Formulating an Opinion

There are certain standards by which a judge should weigh proofs and evidence. The general question of proofs is treated in Book IV, Title X, of the Code. When the proving force of an argument is settled by the law itself the legal rule should be followed. For example, the Code declares that certain kinds of proof are expressly demonstrative.[1] Other proofs are held to be of insufficient or only of partial value.[2]

When the proving force of an argument is left to the discretion of the judge he must follow his conscience, that is, he must sincerely and impartially decide to the best of his ability the value of the arguments presented in the acts and proofs of the case he is considering, and decide whether these arguments are decisive, likely or weak,[3] whether the premises are doubtful, or the inferences illogical, at the same time keeping in mind the quality of the witness and the character of their testimony.[4]

Art. II. Certitude Required of a Judge

Canon 1869, §1, decrees that before a judge passes a sentence he must have in his mind moral certainty concerning the matter which is to be defined by the sentence.

[1] Cfr. cans. 1791, §2, 1747, §1, §2, 1814, 1904, 1972, 2197, §2, §3.

[2] Cfr. cans. 1751, 1758, 1791, §1, 1817, 1826, 1829.

[3] Can. 1789 sq.

[4] Can. 1756 sq.

Moral certitude excludes the probability but not the possibility of error. Moral certitude in the strict sense excludes not only the fear of error but every kind of doubt whether the doubt be great or small, prudent or imprudent. In a wider sense it excludes all fear of error and every serious or prudent doubt but not one or the other slight or imprudent doubt. Moral certitude in the wider sense is all that is required of a judge in forming a sentence, because generally it is the only kind of certitude that one can have, for if a judge would strive to free himself from every slight and baseless suspicion, he would soon be involved in a maze of scruples and perplexities.

This certitude must arise from the acts and proofs offered in the trial, that is from the assertions and negations produced in the trial and juridically proved and recorded in the acts, whether the trial be contentious or criminal. Judges cannot acquire this certitude from things not in the acts or from private knowledge, for as judges they act not as private but as public persons.

What is the duty of the judge when evidence presented in a trial is contrary to his personal or private knowledge? Is a judge so bound by the *acta et probata* that he would have to decide against his own private knowledge?

Three opinions were generally given. The first affirms universally, the second denies universally and the third distinguishes.

The first opinion held by St. Thomas Aquinas,[5] is that a judge should follow the evidence produced and proved in court, since he is a public official and must therefore be guided by the allegations and proofs offered during the trial because public order and respect for the law depend on the good reputation of the courts. If judges could disregard at will the evidence offered, on account of private knowledge they claim to have, the confidence of the public in the integrity of the courts would be shaken, men would take the law in their own hands and peace and order on which the happiness of the community depend would be at an end. He excuses the judge in conscience in sentencing in such a case since he does not intend the evil and acts according to the principle of double effect.

[5] *Summa Theologica* 2. 2, q. 64, art. 6, ad 3.

The second opinion [6] affirms that a judge cannot pronounce sentence against his own conscience, since to do so is to lie, and a lie is intrinsically evil and can never be permitted.

The third opinion which St. Alphonsus considers as probable, distinguishes and holds that a judge can and should pronounce sentence according to the *acta et probata* in contentious causes, and in minor criminal causes, where the punishment to be inflicted is dismissal from office, pecuniary fine and other lesser penalties, but he should acquit in the major criminal cases where one would suffer a grave spiritual or temporal injury.[7]

The opinion of St. Thomas Aquinas seems more conformable to the prescriptions of Canon Law since Canon 1869, §2, declares that ecclesiastical judges must not pass a sentence unless they are certain about the matter of the sentence, and their certainty must be derived from the acts and proofs of the trial. It might be added that if the private knowledge or information of any judge conflicts with knowledge juridically obtained, he can and should make use of his private knowledge in order to examine the testimony more closely so as to discover its defects, or he should endeavor to have the case assigned to another judge. Failing in this, he might in cases involving penalties, inflict the lightest penalty allowed by the law on the case.

It may be asked if a judge can supply proofs?

In private affairs a judge must be disinterested and the parties must plead and defend their own claims save in the cases of minors and those equivalent to minors in law. But in cases involving the good of souls or the public welfare, such as criminal or matrimonial causes, a judge may supply deficiencies in pleading, because he must obtain all the proofs of the plaintiff and the full defense of the defendant.[8]

What is the duty of a judge when after investigation of the acts and proofs of a trial he cannot acquire moral certainty as to the guilt of the defendant in criminal causes, or as to whom the decision should be given in contentious causes?

1. In criminal causes or in a cause where punishment is to be

[6] Ferraris, *Prompta Bibliotheca Canonica,* V. Judex, n. 60.

[7] Bouix, *De Judiciis Ecclesiasticis,* I, p. 140.

[8] Can. 1619.

inflicted, when the guilt of the accused is doubtful, the sentence should be for acquittal; for no one should be condemned unless his guilt is morally certain. When an ecclesiastical judge is not certain that his sentence for the plaintiff will be just he must dismiss the defendant. The Code places the burden of the proof on him who makes an assertion, and it rules that the defendant is to be acquitted if the plaintiff or accuser fails to prove. *Actore non probante, reus absolvitur.*[9] When there is a question of penalties to be inflicted, a person's freedom must be respected unless it is certain that the crime has been perpetrated and prescription has not set in.

Last wills and testaments, the aliment of widows and orphans which in the old law were *causae favorabiles,* are generally treated in the civil courts but if they should be brought to the ecclesiastical court, whatever the civil law decrees in the matter is to be observed by the Church tribunals, except in so far as civil law is contrary to the divine law, or Canon Law rules otherwise.[10]

2. In contentious causes if it is uncertain after investigation for whom the decision should be given:

If the parties are unequal in claim the decision should be for the one whose claim is more weighty. If the arguments are of equal strength, decision should be for the one who has legitimate possession or for the one whose case has the favor of law, or for the party whose case is stronger and more probable. Innocent XI condemned the proposition that a judge may decide for the party whose arguments are less probable.[11]

If both parties are equal in claims the property in dispute should be equally divided among the two contestants or a compromise effected, or if this is impossible, the decision may be given to either one of them unless the Code regulates the matter. The Code prescribes that when there is a doubt as to which one of two competitors has possession, the tribunal may grant it to both of them indivisibly, or require them to place the property in the hands of a sequester until the dispute is settled.[12]

[9] Can. 1748, §2.
[10] Can. 1529. Cf. Cans. 1513 sq.
[11] Denziger, n. 1152.
[12] Can. 1697, §2, §3.

When the defendant has possession with probable title and the plaintiff has the more probable title, the plaintiff should have the decision, because the possession is not certain, or not certainly legitimate, since uncertain possession does not create any presumption of right, and hence the more probable prevails. If the possession is certainly legitimate the common opinion is that the decision should be for the defendant, for certain possession is not overcome by the more probable, but only by certain arguments for the plaintiff.[13]

3. Matrimonial causes are specifically mentioned by the Code as enjoying the favor of law, hence in matrimonial cases when there is a question of validity, and the matter remains doubtful, the sentence must not be against the validity of the marriage.[14] An exception to this general rule regarding doubtful matrimonial cases is found in Canon 1127 where the Code states that in a doubtful matter the Pauline Privilege enjoys the favor of the law.

Art. III. The Interlocutory Sentence

A sentence is interlocutory when it decides an incidental question connected with a cause. Incidental questions of minor character and weight may and usually are settled by a formal decree of the Official or the auditor.[15] The reasons of law and fact for the ruling should be briefly stated in the decree and it should be signed by the Official or the auditor and the notary.[16]

Incidental questions may also be settled in judiciary form either by the Official or the auditor or by the integral tribunal. Questions which have a very direct bearing on the definitive sentence, or which are so intimately connected with the definitive sentence that a decision on them would forestall or amount to the final sentence should be heard by the integral college. When the Official or the auditor or the tribunal as a whole hears an incidental question in a judiciary

[13] Cf. Devoti, *Institutiones Canonicae*, Lib. II, Tit. XIX, n. 6; Reiffenstuel, *Jus Canonicum Universum*, Lib. II, Tit. XIX, IV, 76; Schmalzgrueber, *Jus Ecclesiasticum Universum*, Tom. II, T.T. XXVIII, p. 416.

[14] Can. 1014.

[15] Can. 1840, §1.

[16] Can. 1840, §3.

manner they should proceed as far as possible according to the rules which are laid down for ordinary trials. A petition oral or written is presented, the parties are summoned and heard, and also if necessary the defender of the bond and the promoter of justice. Evidence is presented and the sentence is given in writing and signed by the Official, or the auditor and the notary, or by the three judges if the college as a whole passes on the question.[17] Terms of delay in the hearing of any incidental question should be reduced to the shortest possible time.[18]

An interlocutory sentence may be corrected or revoked for any just reason by the Official or the auditor or the tribunal, either *ex officio* or at the request of one of the parties, provided the other party is heard and also the defender of the bond or the promoter of justice, if they are present.[19]

ART. IV. THE DEFINITIVE SENTENCE

A definitive sentence defines the principal question at issue.

Can. 1871. §1. In tribunali collegiali, qua die et hora iudices ad deliberandum conveniant, collegii praeses constituat; et nisi peculiaris causa aliud suadeat, in ipsa tribunalis sede conventus habeatur.

§2. Assignata conventui die, singuli iudices scriptas afferent conclusiones suas in merito causae, et rationes tam in facto quam in iure, quibus ad conclusionem suam venerint: quae conclusiones actis causae adiungantur, secreto servandae.

§3. Prolatis ex ordine, secundum praecedentiam, ita tamen ut semper a causae ponente seu relatore initium fiat, singulorum conclusionibus, habeatur moderata discussio sub tribunalis praesidis ductu, praesertim ut constabiliatur quid statuendum sit in parte dispositiva sententiae.

[17] Can. 1868.
[18] Can. 1840, §2.
[19] Can. 1841.

§4. In discussione autem fas unicuique est a pristina sua conclusione recedere.

§5. Quod si iudices in prima discussione ad hanc sententiam devenire aut nolint aut nequeant, differri poterit decisio ad novum conventum; qui tamen ultra hebdomadam comperendinari non debet.

A. *The Preparatory Meeting of the Tribunal.*

After the publication of the process and the pleading or the defense has ended, each judge shall receive from the notary a copy of all the acts and proofs of the trial, or in the absence of copies, the original acts and proofs shall be delivered to each judge for study of the case in order that he may prepare his opinion or votum. Canon 1871, §2, requires that on a day and at the hour appointed by the presiding judge of the tribunal, the judges shall meet for deliberation on the sentence. To this meeting each judge shall bring his opinion in writing together with a written statement of the reasons of law and of fact upon which it is based.

At this meeting from which every one else is excluded except the judges, the *ponens* shall briefly outline the case, state the reasons why the cause was introduced, what the plaintiff asks, what the defendant grants or denies, what proofs were introduced, what the conclusions of the litigants are, what incidental questions were settled and the reasons upon which the decisions were based and those which remain to be settled. He shall likewise call attention to any processural defects that may exist.

After giving a summary of the case, the *ponens* shall read his conclusions with the motives of fact and law which prompted them. He shall be followed by the presiding judge and the other judges in order of precedence.[20] A moderate discussion may then follow.

If there are several questions to be settled in the sentence each one is proposed singly to the judges. There should be as many votes taken as there are points to be settled. The sentence of the tribunal is formed by the absolute majority vote of the members.[21] If five

[20] Can. 1873, §3.

[21] Can. 1577, §1.

members of the tribunal are sitting, all five judges must vote and three concurring votes at least are required for the sentence. In a tribunal of three members all shall vote and two concurring votes at least are required for the sentence. If any judge after hearing the conclusions and motives of the other judges wishes to change his vote, he may do so by simply declaring at the end of the document on which his conclusions were given, that he wishes to change his opinion for reasons which he will then express, or he may simply state that he wishes to adhere to the opinion of another judge, naming him, and for the reasons alleged by this other judge in his conclusions. This declaration must be signed by the one who makes it. Attention is called to the fact that these written conclusions are to be preserved with the acts of the case and to be kept secret. They are not to be communicated to the parties, their advocates, the defender of the bond or the promoter of justice or to anyone else except on the order of the judges.

It may be asked whether these conclusions should be sent to the court of appeals, particularly the minority conclusions. The Code is silent on this question. Muniz would seem to infer that they may be sent to the court of appeal.[22] Such action appears to be entirely out of harmony with the legislation of the Code, which says in Canon 1623, §2: "*Tenentur etiam semper ad inviolabile secretum servandum de discussione quae in tribunali collegiali ante ferendam sententiam habetur, tum etiam de variis suffragiis et opinionibus, ibidem prolatis.*" The opinion of the majority or at least those motives which the majority of the tribunal wish incorporated in the sentence, are already in the definitive sentence, and since appeal is made specifically from this sentence, there seems to be no good reason why, in the light of Canon 1632, §2, any more information about the conclusions of the court of first instance than that which is contained in the sentence itself should be required.

1. *The Manner of Voting.* The manner of voting in these closed meetings of the tribunal may be illustrated by a few examples. It is supposed in this instance that the formula of doubt proposed is, *an constet de nullitate matrimonii in casu.* From the acts and

[22] Muniz, *Procedimientos Ecclesiasticos* III, 417 sq.

proofs of the case it may happen that one judge decides that the marriage is invalid *ex metu,* another *ex non impleta conditione,* and the third is of the opinion that the marriage is valid. If the formula was generally proposed the vote of the tribunal should be "*constat de nullitate matrimonii in casu*" because two judges, the absolute majority, were for the nullity.

But if this formula was specific, and read, *an constet de nullitate matrimonii ex metu;* or in the other case, *an constet de nullitate matrimonii ex non impleta conditione;* the sentence would have to read *non constat* in both cases, because in neither of those suppositions was there an absolute majority.

It may happen there will be discordance among the judges about one and the same thing. In a damage suit for example all the judges may agree that the plaintiff is deserving of damages but they cannot agree on the amount to be awarded. One may wish to assess the defendant $100, the second $200, the third $300. The absolute majority in this case would be $200 and this amount must be awarded the plaintiff or an injustice will be done to him unless one of the judges chooses to change his vote.

Aguilar quoted by Roberti [23] is of the opinion that when an absolute majority cannot be had after the second ballot a relative majority will suffice. But this analogy between a moral person [24] and the tribunal does not hold because the collegiate tribunal cannot be considered a moral person. The purpose of the tribunal is not to settle a question arbitrarily but to investigate and carry out the will of the law or the legislator in a given case. Nor can the opinion of those who hold that the presiding judge can cast a decisive vote when the tribunal is deadlocked be held, because this would destroy the very purpose of the legislator in presenting an uneven number of judges for the tribunal.

Muniz [25] and Vidal [26] suggest that when there is a discordance of opinion among a tribunal of three judges and an absolute majority vote cannot be reached, the Ordinary might add two more

[23] *De Processibus,* II, p. 179.

[24] Can. 101, §1, n. 1.

[25] Muniz, *o.c.* III, p. 417.

[26] Wernz-Vidal, VI, p. 545.

judges to the tribunal, since he enjoys this faculty in virtue of Canon 1576, §2. This could not be done if five judges were already hearing the case. They also suggest, following the practice of the Rota, that recourse might be had in such a contingency to the Ordinary, to have a new turn or section of the tribunal substituted.

What is to be done, since the Code requires an unequal number of judges,[27] when a college of three or five judges is hearing say an exception of suspicion against one of their own number, and the vote ends in a tie, one voting for the judge in question and the other against him, or in a tribunal of five judges if two vote to uphold the exception and two to reject it? This may be solved on the principle "*actore non probante reus absolvitur.*" Since a majority is required in either case, and it is wanting, the defendant should be absolved of the suspicion because with two votes for and two votes against the defendant, the case of the plaintiff cannot be held as proved since a majority has not been reached; therefore, the charge of suspicion cannot be upheld.

Canon 1871, §5, declares that if the judges cannot reach a decision or are unwilling to do so they may hold another discussion on the case but it must be held not later than eight days after the first session.

From these opinions or *vota* the *ponens* must formulate the definitive sentence, and in drafting the sentence of the tribunal he should incorporate the opinions of the majority.[28]

B. *Contents of the Sentence*

The sentence must settle the controversy at issue, that is be absolutory or condemnatory concerning the question contained in the formula or the libellus and suitable answers should be given to each disputed point in the libellus. It must be in no way conditional but determine as far as the nature of the case permits what the condemned party must give, do, take upon himself, suffer or refrain from, and also in what manner and at what place and time the obligation is to be fulfilled. It shall likewise contain the motives *in*

[27] Can. 1576, §2.
[28] Can. 1584.

facto and *in jure* on which the decisive part of the sentence is based.[29]

Like all sentences, the sentence of the collegiate tribunal shall in the beginning contain an invocation of the Divine Name. It must state in the following order the names of the judges, the plaintiff and defendant, procurators, together with their domiciles, the defender of the bond and the promoter of justice if they have taken part in the trial. A statement of the assessment of the expenses of the trial is also to be expressed in the sentence.

It shall close with the date and place when and where the sentence was drafted, and the signatures of all the judges and the notary. A sentence passed by a board of judges but signed only by the presiding judge and the notary is invalid.[30]

[29] Can. 1873.

[30] Pont. Com. Int. Cod., July 14, 1922. *A.A.S.* XIV (1922), 528.

PART III

PROCEDURE IN MATRIMONIAL CAUSES PROPER TO THE DIOCESAN COLLEGIATE TRIBUNAL OF FIRST INSTANCE

CHAPTER VI

PRELIMINARY NOTIONS

ART. I. DEFINITION AND KINDS OF MATRIMONIAL CAUSES

A matrimonial cause is any question or dispute in a matrimonial matter that is submitted to the authoritative judgment of an ecclesiastical judge. A matrimonial cause in a strict sense deals with the validity or nullity of the marriage bond. Specifically matrimonial causes in the strict sense embrace all disputes as to the validity or invalidity of the bond due to the existence of diriment impediments, lack of consent or defect in the required form, the declaration of the fact of consummation or non-consummation of the marriage,[1] perpetual separation,[2] the verification of conditions requisite for the application of the Pauline Privilege,[3] the rights and obligations necessarily inherent in the marriage contract,[4] and the legitimacy of offspring.[5]

Matrimonial causes in a broad sense include questions of the separable affects of the marriage bond, such as inheritance, dowry, etc.

Questions concerning the validity, liceity and effects of betrothal also come under the class of matrimonial causes,[6] but judicial action to demand the fulfillment of the contract is denied by Canon Law.[7] Crimes against marriage such as abortion, rape and abduction, bigamy, adultery and concubinage are to be classed as criminal rather than as matrimonial causes, and while the ecclesiastical court is competent in these matters, Ordinaries should not as a rule pro-

[1] Cans. 1119; 1015, §2; 1970 sq.

[2] Can. 1130.

[3] Can. 1121, §2.

[4] Can. 1111.

[5] Cans. 1114; 1117; 1051.

[6] Can. 1553, §1, n. 1.

[7] Cans. 1017, §3; 1667, Pont. Com. Int. Cod., June 2-3, 1918. *A.A.S.* X (1918), 345.

ceed against a culprit, if he is a lay person, since the secular court by proceeding against him has sufficiently safeguarded the public welfare [8]

A judicial process may be necessary to establish the freedom of a person to marry if there was a previous marriage or this may be treated by way of an administrative investigation.[9] The question of the presumed death of a former spouse can be decided judicially or extrajudicially.[10] Temporary separation can likewise be effected extrajudicially.[11]

Canon 1960 states that the Catholic Church is the only competent judge of the marriages of those baptized. It follows from this, that all marriages between baptized persons, whether Catholics or not, belong to her jurisdiction, consequently mixed marriages, and marriages of heretics. The Church, however, does not choose to judge of marriages between non-Catholics, except when asked, or when it is in the interest of Catholics to do so. Marriages between non-baptized persons (infidels, Jews, etc.) may be subject indirectly to the forum of the Church by title of connected cause.

The marriages of infidels are not subject to the judgment of the Church as long as at least one of the parties is not converted to the Christian faith and has not received baptism.

The competence of the Church extends to all that concerns the marriage bond, the spiritual effects, the inseparable temporal effects and the canonical consequences.

With regard to the civil effects of marriage such as the dowry, inheritance, gifts, etc., if such effects are the principal point at issue, it belongs rather to the civil judge to pass judgment on them,[12] but if they are incidental or accessory to a cause on the validity or licitness of marriage, the ecclesiastical judge is competent to try and decide such points.[13] Crimes against marriage and cases of broken espousals are best left to the civil courts.

[8] Cans. 1933, §3; 2223, §3, n. 3.
[9] Can. 1019; cf. 1567; *AkKR.* CV (1925), 113.
[10] Can. 1053; Cappello, *De Sacramentis* III, n. 434; *A.A.S.* II (1909), 198.
[11] Can. 1131, §1.
[12] Can. 1016.
[13] Can. 1961.

Practically all matrimonial causes brought to the ecclesiastical courts today are reducible to three classes; those which concern 1. the validity or nullity of the contract; 2. declaration of the fact of non-consummation; 3. perpetual separation.[14]

This study is concerned only with those which fall within the first class.

Art. II. Matrimonial Causes Proper to the Collegiate Tribunal

Canonists [15] group the contentious cases concerning the bond under three headings. Those arising: (1) from disability of the contracting parties,[16] (2) from defective consent,[17] and (3) from defective form.[18]

[14] Vermeersch-Creusen, *Epitome* III, n. 276.

[15] Lanier, *Guide Pratique,* XVIII, sqq.; Fornier, *Le Mariage chretin,* p. 343.

[16] Cfr. cans. 1059, 1067, 1068, 1069, 1070, 1072, 1073, 1074, 1075, 1076, 1077, 1078, 1079. Prior to the Code—illicit affinity.

[17] Cfr. cans. 1082, 1083, 1086, §2, 1087, 1092.

[18] Cfr. 1015, §3, 1088, §1, 1094. Before the decree *Ne Temere,* August 2, 1907, in force April 19, 1908, in every place where *Tametsi* had been promulgated, defective form arises from marriages of baptized persons that were not contracted before the pastor of the domicile or quasi-domicile of one of the parties.

After the Ne Temere (April 19, 1908), defective form arises from marriages not contracted before the pastor or Ordinary of the place where the marriage takes place or before a priest delegated by the pastor or Ordinary.

Three situations worthy of mention here were presented to the Pontifical Commission for the Interpretation of the Code:

1. Two Catholics in a place subject to the Tridentine decree *Tametsi,* and after the decree *Ne Temere* went into effect, contracted marriage either before an heretical minister or a civil magistrate, having obtained a civil divorce, wish to marry *in facie ecclesiae.*

2. A Catholic and a non-Catholic contracted marriage in a Protestant church either in a place subject to the *Tametsi* to which the Benedictine declaration had not been extended, or after the *Ne Temere,* having obtained a civil divorce, now wishes to marry a Catholic before the Church.

3. Apostates from the faith, married each other before a non-Catholic minister or before a civil magistrate, obtained a divorce and returned to the faith, and now wish to contract another marriage before the Church.

The Pontifical Commission in a decree issued October 16, 1919, declared

By virtue of Canon 1990 when a declaration of nullity is sought on the grounds of disparity of cult, orders, solemn vow of chasity, valid marriage bond, consanguinity, affinity or spiritual relationship, these cases can be judged according to the summary procedure.[19]

that these three cases did not require any judiciary procedure or even the intervention of the Defender of the Bond, but could be decided by the Ordinary or by the pastor consulting the Ordinary—in short by establishing an inquiry as to the free status of the parties concerned. Cfr. A.A.S., XI (1919), 479. The marriages of divorced Catholics who have attempted a civil marriage are to be considered as non-existent and require no procedure. A.A.S. (1919), 479. A marriage invalid by reason of the impediment of age while not mentioned in Canon 1990 would seem to come under this process, if the existence of the impediment could be established from a baptismal record, or birth certificate. To establish the fact that a dispensation was never granted it is sufficient to consult the parish or chancery records. Cfr. Vermeersch-Creusen, *Epitome* III, n. 296; Lanier, *Guide Pratique de la Procedure Matrimoniale*, p. 6; Wernz-Vidal, *Jus Canonicum* V, n. 705. Lanier is of the opinion that if a marriage case is presented in which a declaration of nullity is sought on the grounds of pre-code clandestinity and the nullity is evident, the Ordinary may be contented with a summary procedure provided the marriage was contracted before April 19, 1908.

[19] In this administrative procedure documents provide the principal and basic proof, but it may comprise, if there is need, the hearing of certain persons. In order that the Ordinary can proceed in this way, the following conditions must be present or realized.

Conditions required: 1. That the nullity must be founded on the existence of one of the impediments enumerated in Canon 1990, and of *these only* viz., impediments of disparity of cult,—order,—solemn vow of chastity,—the bond,—consanguinity, affinity, or of spiritual relationship.

2. The nullity must be *evident,* that is such that it can be proved by a document. a. Certain—having to do exactly with some particular impediment and some particular person. b. Authentic—either the original or a certified copy of the original and having the desired signatures. c. That it is not liable to any contradiction—to any exception or to any suspicion of error in itself or its adjuncts.

3. That the existence of the impediment and the absence of a dispensation at the time of the marriage be established with an equal certitude. The Pontifical Commission for the Authentic Interpretation of the Code declared on June 16, 1931, that equal certitude required by Canon 1990 can be had not only from a certain and authentic document but also through other legitimate proofs. (*A.A.S.*, XXIII [1931], 353.)

When these conditions are realized the Ordinary should: a. Call the two

When a declaration of nullity is sought in any contentious cause concerning the bond, provided it is not removed from the competence of the Diocesan court and not mentioned in Canon 1990, the Ordi-

parties, for one cannot effectively treat of a marriage without the two interested parties being notified of it. b. Hear the Defender of the bond. c. Declare juridically the nullity of the marriage.

The Brief. It will, in this procedure, be necessary to draw up a brief containing the data necessary for the case. Certificates of the civil marriage, and of the religious marriage, documents which establish the existence of the impediment; certificates showing the relationship which joins the two parties, certificates of baptism, letter of ordination or of a solemn profession, testimony of various episcopal curias, that such and such dispensation has not been accorded, are required. Moreover, it will be well, although not necessary, to gather in the brief the depositions of each of the parties, following a questionnaire prepared in advance.

Role of the Defender of the Bond. It happens sometimes that certain doubts present themselves in the course of the inquiry, for example with regard to the existence of the impediment or the concession of the dispensation. If these doubts continue, the Defender of the bond, who in every case should intervene, is bound to appeal to the judge of the second instance (to the Ordinary, and not to the Official as such). The acts will be transmitted to him and he will be notified that the case in question is exempted from the formalities of an ordinary trial (C. 1091). The judge of the second instance will decide with the intervention *only* of the Defender of the bond—always following the administrative mode—whether the decision of the first instance is to be confirmed, or whether it is necessary to have recourse to the normal procedure. In this latter case, the brief will be returned to the judge of the first instance, who will turn the case over to the Official to be tried by the collegiate tribunal (C. 1992).

Sentence or Simple Declaration. Canon 1992 speaks of a sentence rendered (*utrum sententia sit confirmanda*), while 1990 uses the expression *declarare.* One might ask if the Ordinary shall give a sentence properly so called? It seems that a simply motivated declaration will suffice. The judge, nevertheless, should be guided in drawing up this declaration by the prescriptions of Canon 1874, especially in the exposition of motives which prove the evidence of the nullity of the marriage in question. A certificate of the free status can then be given to each of the two interested parties, or at least, to one of them, for if the marriage was declared null because of the impediment of the bond (previous marriage), it is clear that the party already bound would have no right to receive this certificate of free status.

For a more extensive treatment of the administrative or documentary process the reader is referred to Lanier, *Guide Pratique,* p. 1 sq.; Kay, Competence in Matrimonial Procedure, p. 109 sq.

nary must appoint a Collegiate Tribunal of three judges to try the case and the decision can not be rendered except by all of the judges voting on the sentence. The majority decide what sentence is to be given. Causes which may be tried according to the summary process mentioned in Canon 1990, in which recourse is had to the Judge of second instance and which still remain doubtful shall be referred back to the court of first instance to be tried by the Collegiate Tribunal.[20] By virtue of Canon 1576, §2 any other matrimonial cause which presents special difficulties or which is important by reason of time, parties or circumstances involved may also be entrusted to the Collegiate Tribunal.

Art. III. The Tribunal in Contentious Causes Involving the Bond of Marriage

The Collegiate Tribunal in these contentious causes involving the bond of marriage must be composed of three judges for every case on trial and no contrary privilege or custom may be claimed to off-set this law.[21] Other persons in addition to the judges who must take part in these trials are the defender of the marriage bond and the notary, and in certain causes the promoter of justice. The rights and duties of each of these officers will be briefly explained in this article.

(a) *Rights and Duties of the Defender of the Bond in Matrimonial Causes.* In all matrimonial causes reserved to the collegiate tribunal the defender of the bond has the right and duty to intervene, and to uphold with diligence the validity of the marriage bond by the use of every lawful means.

(1) *Rights.* The defender of the bond has the right at any stage of the trial to inspect the acts of the case even before the publication of the process.[22] He may demand that the points at issue be more clearly defined.[23] He must be heard in recourse to the superior

[20] Can. 1992.
[21] Can. 1576, §1, n. 4.
[22] Can. 1969, §1.
[23] Can. 1729, §4.

court on the rejection of the bill of complaint.[24] He may seek a declaration of contumacy against the plaintiff or the defendant and prosecute the charge.[25] He has the right to be informed of all proofs and allegations presented in the case so that he may prepare his objections. He can demand that witnesses be summoned or that those already heard be recalled and re-examined, or that new witnesses be introduced even after the publication of the process.[26] He has the right to ask for more time in order to prepare his questions, objections and other writings in defense of the marriage, and this extension should ordinarily be granted him by the tribunal.[27] Acts that he suggests must be made, unless the unanimous vote of the tribunal is against him.[28] He is to be heard on the correction or revocation of interlcutory sentences.[29] A definitive sentence should not be passed by the tribunal unless the defender has formally declared that he has nothing more to bring forward. This is presumed if he has not done so before the day set by the tribunal for the sentence.[30] He may introduce the *querela nullitatis*.[31]

(2) *Duties*. It is the duty of the defender of the bond to assist at the examination of the parties, witnesses, and experts, to examine documents, to hand to the presiding judge interrogatories in a sealed envelope to be opened only in the act of examination, to suggest if he thinks it necessary new questions during the examination, to weigh the arguments advanced by the parties, witnesses and experts and to answer them.[32]

If the sentence of the tribunal was for the nullity of the marriage whether the defendant appeals or not, it is the duty *ex officio* of the defender to appeal the case within *ten days*. If he neglects to do so the tribunal may compel him to do so, since the defender of the bond

[24] Can. 1709, §3.
[25] Can. 1850, §2.
[26] Can. 1969, §3.
[27] Can. 1969, §3.
[28] Can. 1969, §4.
[29] Can. 1841.
[30] Can. 1984, §1, n. 2.
[31] Can. 1897, §1.
[32] Can. 1968.

may not agree to a judgment of nullity unless it has been affirmed by a twofold sentence.[33]

If the sentence of the tribunal was for the validity of the marriage he need not appeal, although the parties may do so. The duty of the defender to appeal in courts of second instance is not properly within the scope of this section of the dissertation.

An interesting question suggests itself here, namely whether the defender of the marriage bond has any right to demand the conclusions, especially the minority opinion, arrived at by the judges of the tribunal in formulating the sentence. It seems not. He has the right to inspect the acts of the trial at any stage of the proceedings [34] and is entitled to be heard last,[35] and the tribunal cannot proceed to render a verdict unless the defender has formally declared upon request, that he has nothing more to bring forward or to inquire into,[36] but it seems with this declaration his duty is suspended until the sentence has been passed, when his is the right to appeal the sentence. He does not participate in that secret session which judges hold before passing sentence. In view of the prescriptions of Canon 1623, §2, which bind the judges and all officials of the court to absolute secrecy concerning the discussion and various votes and opinions of the judges, it would seem that he has done his full and sufficient duty by considering in his appeal only the motives contained in the sentence itself.

(b) *The Notary.* At every trial there must be present a notary who acts as secretary or clerk, and the acts are invalid unless they are drawn up by him or at least subscribed by him.[37] The

[33] Can. 1986.

[34] Can. 1968, §1.

[35] Can. 1984, §1.

[36] Can. 1984, §2.

[37] Can. 1585, §1. Two exceptions to this general law are:

1. The *Regulae Servandae* issued by the Sacred Congregation of Sacraments, May 7, 1923, to be observed in processes *super matrimonio rato et non consummato*—*A. A. S.* XV (1923), 397, n. 24, §4—states that if the *judex delegatus* finds himself in a territory where there is no notary available, he should make a note of this fact in the document, and this document even though not signed by a notary is worthy of belief.

2. The mandate of a procurator when the *mandans* is unable to write, in the absence of a notary, may be signed by the pastor or two witnesses. The fact of his inability to write must be noted in the document: Can. 1659, §2.

Chancellor of a diocese is a notary *ex officio.*[38] Besides the Chancellor or Vice-chancellor there should be appointed other ecclesiastical notaries who may act in all judicial affairs or in a certain case or a certain class of cases as the Bishop deems proper.[39] Where there is a lack of priests, laymen may be appointed notaries in matrimonial causes.[40] Whoever is appointed must be a man of good reputation, and beyond suspicion concerning character and trustworthiness.[41] Unless the Bishop has appointed a notary for a case, the presiding judge of the tribunal must select a notary from among those approved by the Bishop. By way of exception, if the witness who is to be examined lives so far away from the court that it would be very expensive for him to come to court, the judge may send the questions to be asked of the witness to a worthy priest who lives near the place, and he will examine the witness with the aid of another person who will act as notary.[42]

The office of notary is strictly territorial[43] but an instrument validly drawn up by a notary constitutes of itself full proof for what it asserts not only in the place where it was made but everywhere. The notary takes the oath *de officio rite et fideliter implendo*[44] either before the Ordinary or his delegate, or before the presiding judge or his delegate. His oath of office always implies that he must keep inviolable the secret of his office.[45] An exception against the notary is heard by the presiding judge. This office is incompatible with any other in the court.

A notary may be removed or suspended from office by him who constituted him, or by his successor or superior. The Vicar Capitular or Administrator needs the consent of the chapter or the consultors to remove a notary.[46] A judge for a just cause may remove or suspend a notary whom he has assumed for a particular cause.

[38] Can. 372, §3.
[39] Can. 373, §1, n. 2.
[40] Can. 373, §3.
[41] Can. 373, §4.
[42] Can. 1770, §2, n. 4.
[43] Can. 374, n. 2.
[44] Can. 1621, §1.
[45] Can. 1623, §1, §2, §3.
[46] Can. 373, §5.

It is the duty of the notary to reduce to writing all the acts of the trial, both the *acta causae* and the *acta processus.*

He should be present at every session of the trial and all the acts of the trial should be drawn up or at least subscribed by him.[47] He should also sign each page of the acts, and stamp each page with the seal proper to the tribunal. The notary shall assist at the taking of the oath by the officers of the tribunal if they are constituted permanently or at the beginning of the trial if they are appointed for one case only, and shall make a record of this fact.[48] If the parties appear before the tribunal of their own accord without being summoned the notary shall make a note of this fact in the acts.[49] He shall, with the judge or his auditor, sign the citations and seal them with the seal of the tribunal.[50] He shall add the report of the messenger in serving the citations, or the receipt if the citations were made by registered mail, to the acts of the case.[51]

He reduces to writing all petitions orally proposed, reads them to the party and gets his signature.[52] He takes down the address of residence at which the parties and their advocates or procurators wish to receive communications from the court.[53] He writes down when orally proposed the mandates of procurators and advocates,[54] the oaths of the parties, witnesses and experts, the questions of the judges and the answers of the parties, witnesses and experts,[55] making note in the document of anything that happened during the hearings which he thinks worthy of mention.[56] When an expert gives his opinion orally it must be taken down immediately by the notary and signed by him and the expert.[57] The notary should seriously refrain from infringing on the duties of the judges of the tribunal, such

[47] Can. 1585.
[48] Can. 1621.
[49] Can. 1711, §2.
[50] Can. 1715, §2.
[51] Can. 1722, §2.
[52] Can. 1707, §3.
[53] Can. 1708.
[54] Can. 1659, §3.
[55] Cans. 1773, §1; 1770, §2, n. 4.
[56] Cans. 1779; 1745.
[57] Can. 1801, §1.

as examining witnesses, rendering interlocutory sentences, etc. *"Videat, audiat, taceat."* He takes down the relations of those who make the local inspection mentioned in Canons 1806-1811 and keeps a careful record of the day and hour when the inspection was held, what was said or done during the inspection, and what was decreed by the judge. This record must be signed by the judge or the one who made the inspection in his place and by the notary. The sentence published by the tribunal he must also take down in writing.

As each act is completed the notary will read the act in the presence of the party examined and the judges, then obtain the signature of the presiding judge of tribunal and of the witness, and sign the document himself. Every time the sessions are adjourned this fact must be noted, and the document must be signed at the notation by the presiding judge of the tribunal and the notary.[58] When the signature of the parties, witnesses or experts is required on any act and they are unable or unwilling to sign their name, a notation to this effect must be made in the document, and the notary and the judge shall attest that the act was read to the respective parties, witnesses or experts and that they were unable or unwilling to sign.[59] The notary with the presiding judge also signs all decrees, citations, notifications, all interlocutory sentences.[60]

If with the permission of the tribunal a moderate oral discussion or pleading takes place, the notary shall take down as much of the discussion as the judges command, or either party with the consent of the judges demands.[61] The notary together with the judges of the tribunal signs the definitive sentence, and he notes at the end of the sentence, the date and place where it was drafted.[62] If an appeal from the sentence is made, the notary shall make note of it in the acts; if the appeal is made orally before the tribunal, he shall put it down in writing.[63] A notary can never be compelled to testify concerning matters which he knows only by reason of, and in connection

[58] Can. 1643, §2.

[59] Can. 1643.

[60] Cans. 1715, §2; 1874, §5.

[61] Can. 1866, §2, §4.

[62] Can. 1874, §5.

[63] Can. 1882, §1.

with his office, when the revelation of the knowledge sought, would in any way violate the secret of his office.[64]

The notary may likewise act as secretary of the tribunal and may receive in the name of the tribunal all writings directed to the tribunal, all petitions, documents to be exhibited by the parties, the written relations of experts, the animadversions of the defender of the bond and the promoter of justice, the defense and reply of the advocates and procurators, and in courts of appeal the acts of the courts of preceding instances.

The notary makes, or at least attests the fidelity of all copies of judicial documents issued by order of the presiding judge.[65] He attends to sending of citations, notifications of witnesses, transmits the defense and replies to the members of the tribunal, the parties, their advocates or procurators, the promoter of justice and the defender of the bond, and sees to the publication and printing of the process where this is prescribed by the tribunal. At the close of the trial the notary will return to the parties such documents as the presiding judge orders him to return. The documents which remain should be deposited in the archives of the tribunal or in the absence of these in the diocesan archives at the chancery, either the secret or public archives, according to the contents of the documents. These documents should be arranged in an orderly fashion, indexed and catalogued in booklet form.

If the case is appealed, the notary shall forward to the tribunal of appeal a complete transcript of the original acts arranged in booklet form, paged and indexed, together with the attestation that the copy is a faithful and complete transcript of the original text.[66] These acts may be returned by the appeal court if they are not in proper form, and the notary through whose negligence this happened is bound to have them corrected and forwarded at his own expense.[67] The notary is forbidden to furnish copies of judicial acts and documents without an order from the Official.[68]

[64] Can. 1775, §2, n. 1.
[65] Can. 1645, §3.
[66] Can. 1644, §1, §2.
[67] Can. 1644.
[68] Can. 1645.

The notary may be appointed by the tribunal custodian of any money deposited to cover the expenses of the trial or posted as security that the parties concerned will abide by the decision of the tribunal.[69]

(c) *The Promoter of Justice.* The Promoter of Justice has the duty of appearing in all criminal causes and in those civil causes in which in the judgment of the Ordinary the public welfare is at stake.[70] It is his duty to file and prosecute certain matrimonial cases. In this latter capacity only is the promoter of justice considered in this article. Whenever a marriage is null because of an impediment public by nature, the promoter of justice must *ex officio* attack this marriage if the parties are unwilling or unable to take the necessary steps to secure a declaration of nullity. Certain persons have not the right to attack a marriage.[71] They may, however, denounce a marriage to the Ordinary or promoter of justice. The latter assumes the function of plaintiff and presents the case to the tribunal and prosecutes it.[72]

[69] Cans. 1909, §2; 1626.
[70] Can. 1586, §2.
[71] Cfr. Can. 1971, §1, §2.
[72] Can. 1971, §3. Cfr. p. 99 sq.

CHAPTER VII

INTRODUCTION OF A CAUSE

ART. I. PRELIMINARY INVESTIGATION

THE introduction of a matrimonial cause to the diocesan tribunal is usually preceded by an interview or consultation with some priest. In advising a person who seeks a declaration of nullity of a marriage, one must act prudently and cautiously in order to avoid giving false hopes of relief.

Canonists recognize three great sources of nullity in marriage:

1. The contractants were incapable of entering the contract.
2. The consent was not valid.
3. The substantial form prescribed by law was not followed.

If the contractants were incapable of contracting a valid marriage because of a diriment impediment which could not or was not removed, if there was a defect in consent, or if there was a lack or defect in the substantial form of marriage, then the Church will juridically speaking, not annul a marriage but will declare it null *ab initio* or non existing. But if at the moment of marriage, the marriage was valid because it was not vitiated by any of these defects, the marriage is valid forever.

A priest consulted in regard to a declaration of nullity on a marriage should deal with the parties concerned. If from this preliminary investigation, he has good reasons to suspect the invalidity of the marriage, he should endeavor to effect a reconciliation between the parties and convalidation of the marriage. If he finds lack of consent or a defect in consent, he should try to induce the party, whose consent is asserted to have been deficient, to renew the consent. If the reason for having the marriage declared invalid is the lack of the prescribed form he should make an effort to have the consent renewed in the form prescribed. If the marriage was invalid because of a diriment impediment which can be removed or from which the Church dispenses, such as crime, public honesty, spiritual relationship, etc., dispensation should be sought and the marriage convalidated. If the impediment is such that it cannot be removed, or if the priest is unsuccessful in his efforts to effect a reconciliation, or convalidation, only then should he suggest recourse to the ecclesiastical court. The Church places this obligation of avoiding judgments on the tribunal, but it is generally too late to accomplish the desired results, when the case has been brought to the attention of the diocesan curia.[1] Pastors and confessors have a better opportunity of effecting a convalidation, but their efforts in this matter do not regularly excuse the judges of the tribunal from this grave obligation of the law.

Supposing that it is impossible to effect a reconciliation between the parties, the next step in the process, is the introduction of the cause to the tribunal.

Art. II. The Bill of Complaint or Libellus

The bill of complaint is a statement of the case made to a competent judge with a request for relief.

Can. 1970.—Tribunal collegiale nullam causam matrimonialem cognoscere vel definire potest, nisi regularis accusatio vel iure facta petitio praecesserit.

Canon 1970 declares that the collegiate tribunal cannot take cognizance of, nor decide, any matrimonial cause unless a regular accusation or legal petition is presented.

The "*accusatio*" or regular accusation takes place when one of the parties attacks the validity of the marriage against the other party who asserts that it is valid, or who is unwilling to have it attacked. A petition (*petitio*) is used when both parties agree to ask for a declaration of nullity. A matrimonial cause may likewise be introduced by denunciation. Every Catholic is allowed to denounce, not accuse, the nullity of a marriage to the Ordinary or the promoter of justice, and the latter shall then proceed against the marriage *ex officio*.

In formulating the bill of complaint (*supplex libellus*), the parties

[1] Can. 1965.

may invoke the aid of a priest or of the Official or one of the approved advocates. The accusation or petition should be presented in writing but if the plaintiff is illiterate or unable to write, the Official may permit it to be made orally in his presence and shall command the notary of the tribunal to put the oral petition in writing, and to read it to the plaintiff so that he may approve of it.[2]

The bill (*libellus*) should contain:

1. The name of the tribunal before which the case is to be tried.[3]

2. The object of the plea—what is asked of the court. If the petition asks that the marriage be declared invalid because of a diriment impediment it should set forth that the marriage in question was contracted by so and so at such a time, and in such a place, and before such a priest; that at the time of the marriage a diriment impediment, or some other invalidating defect stood in the way of the marriage, and was not removed. The impediment should be described. If it is claimed the marriage is invalid because fear and violence existed at the time of the marriage, the acts of violence should be described, and the names of those who can support this contention should be indicated. The demand for a declaration of nullity should be clearly and distinctly expressed.

The certificate of the marriage should be sent with the petition, and also the baptismal certificates of the parties. The present matrimonial status of the parties in the eyes of the state, should also be expressed in the petition, and the decree of civil divorce should be presented if such a divorce has been obtained.

3. The name of the defendant and address if known.

4. The reasons of law on which the plea is based, at least in a general way.[4]

5. The signature of the plaintiff, his advocate or procurator, the date (day, month, year), and the place where the plaintiff, attorney or procurator resides, and where they will be ready to receive the judicial acts.[5]

The commission of the advocate and the mandate of the pro-

[2] Can. 1707, §1, §3

[3] Can. 1708, §1.

[4] Can. 1708, §2.

[5] Can. 1708, §3.

curator may be deposited with the tribunal at this time. From a practical viewpoint this is the most convenient time to introduce the names of witnesses who are expected to be called.

Having received the *libellus,* the next step in the process is the acceptance or rejection of the *libellus.* The tribunal shall, 1. examine its own competency; 2. the right of the parties to attack the marriage.

Art. III. Competency of the Tribunal

The diocesan collegiate tribunal is absolutely incompetent [6] in matrimonial causes of rulers,[7] and in causes legitimately brought to the Holy See in first instance.[8] Matrimonial causes involving a papal dispensation from a ratified but non-consummated marriage are reserved to the Sacred Congregation of the Sacraments.[9] No inferior tribunal can institute proceedings of this kind without the permission of the Holy See. If in a trial conducted to establish the nullity of a marriage on account of the impediment of impotence, the non-consummation of the marriage rather than impotence is proved, the diocesan collegiate tribunal should stop the proceedings and forward all the acts of the case to the Sacred Congregation of the Sacraments.[10] In this case if the proofs of non-consummation seem incomplete or insufficient, the judge may without having recourse to Rome, complete the acts in the case before sending the cause to Rome.[11] Involved cases of the Pauline Privilege as well as permission to omit the interpellations, must be submitted to the Sacred Congregation of the Holy Office.[12]

The local Ordinary can verify in a summary investigation or in a judicial fashion through the diocesan curia [13] the existence of the conditions necessary for the application of the Pauline Privilege,

[6] Can. 1892, §1.
[7] Can. 1558.
[8] Cans. 1559, §2; 1569, 1597.
[9] Can. 1963, §1.
[10] Can. 1963, §2.
[11] S. C. de Sacr., Instr., May 7, 1923, reg. 3—*A.A.S.*, XV (1923), 389 sq.
[12] Can. 1121, §1.
[13] Cf. Can. 1122, §1. Perries, *Procédure Canonique,* p. 224.

viz., a. a valid marriage contracted between two infidels (can. 1120); b. the reception of baptism by one party (can. 1121 §1); c. the refusal of conversion or, at least, of peaceful cohabitation on the part of the unbaptized party when asked by the baptized party prior to the second marriage which will sever the former bond (cans. 1121, §1, 1122, 1126). Cases beyond the scope of the Pauline Privilege involving the exercise of Papal authority must be referred to the Apostolic See for decision. The diocesan court cannot validly accept matrimonial causes of a judicial nature, in which the actor is a non-Catholic without securing in each case permission of the Holy Office. Cases of an administrative character may be received without this permission.[14]

Without the permission of the Holy See, certain Catholics are juridically incapable of becoming actors in matrimonial causes. These persons are Catholics who have been wittingly responsible for the impediment from which the nullity of the marriage arose.[15] Impediment in Canon 1971, §1, n. 1 is to be understood not only of the diriment impediments strictly so called[16] but also of diriment impediments improperly so called.[17] Hence it does not matter whether the invalidity arose from a diriment impediment, or from a deliberate lack of consent (error, force and fear, condition) or a defect of the prescribed form, those who through malice or neglect have caused the invalidity of the marriage are forbidden to sue for a declaration of nullity.[18]

If the cause is one which may be treated by the diocesan tribunal, the next question to be settled is whether the cause is proper to this particular tribunal.

Can. 1964.—In aliis causis matrimonialibus iudex competens est iudex loci in quo matrimonium celebratum est aut in quo pars conventa vel, si una sit acatholica, pars catholica domicilium vel quasi-domicilium habet.

[14] S. C. S. Off., Jan. 17, 1928—*A.A.S.*, XX (1928), 75.

[15] Can. 1971, §1, n. 1.

[16] Cans. 1067; 1080.

[17] Cans. 1081, 1103.

[18] Pont. Com. Int. Cod., Mar. 12, 1929—*A.A.S.*, XXI (1929), 171.

Canon 1964 states that in matrimonial causes which are proper to the diocesan court, the competent judge or tribunal is the judge or tribunal of the place in which the marriage was contracted, or of the place in which the defendant has a domicile or quasi-domicile, unless the defendant is a non-Catholic in which event the domicile or quasi-domicile of the Catholic party determines the proper tribunal. The general rule that the forum of the defendant (*reus*) is preferred, and in case of a multiplicity of proper courts, the plaintiff (*actor*) has the choice of the forum, is applicable only in matrimonial cases where both parties are Catholics. The judge of the diocese of contract and the judge of the diocese of domicile and quasi-domicile are equally competent, and if the court of the diocese of contract is chosen no distinction is made whether both parties are Catholics or not.

Canon 1964 considers a marriage which is attacked by one of the parties. What diocesan tribunal is competent when there is a question of a Catholic wishing to contract a marriage with one who has been previously married? Since the Ordinary of the Catholic party has the duty of establishing the freedom of his subject,[19] he is competent to make the judicial inquiry into the validity of any previous marriage by title of connected cause.[20]

If the person whom the Catholic party wishes to marry is a non-Catholic and was involved in a previous marriage with a non-Catholic, who is to become actor and what diocesan court is to try the case? The Catholic party is certainly not the "*pars catholica*" spoken of in Canon 1971, §1, who is capable of accusing a marriage for he is not a party to that marriage. There is the further difficulty of admitting a non-Catholic as actor. If permission of the Holy Office is obtained for the non-Catholic party to act as *actor,* the Ordinary of the Catholic party who is entitled to make the investigation about the freedom of his subject to marry, is capable of hearing such a cause by title of connected cause. Without permission of the Holy See no diocesan court is competent in such a case.[21] If one of the parties to this non-Catholic marriage had in the meantime be-

[19] Can. 1019 sq.

[20] Can. 1567; *AkKR,* CV (1925), 113.

[21] *Jus Pontificium,* VI (1926), 159.

come a Catholic, the Ordinary of the place where the marriage was contracted is competent to undertake the cause. The Ordinary of the Catholic party wishing to contract marriage with the convert, may also undertake to settle the question of the validity of the first marriage by title of connected cause. The convert party of the first marriage may by Canon 1964 seek a decision in either the forum of contract or the forum of domicile or quasi-domicile.[22]

A. *The Forum of Contract.* The Code in Canon 1964 admits without qualification the competence of the court of the place where the marriage has been contracted to cite the parties even if they are not within the territorial jurisdiction of this court. The forum of contract is applicable only where the marriage has taken place,[23] but not where the new marriage is to be contracted.[24]

B. *The Forum of Domicile and Quasi-Domicile.* The local tribunal obtains competence in matrimonial causes by reason of diocesan domicile or quasi-domicile of the married parties.[25] A domicile supposes either residence in a diocese with the intention of staying there permanently unless something calls one away, or residence in a diocese that has extended over ten complete years.[26] A quasi-domicile is acquired by residence in a diocese with the intention to stay there for the greater part of a year, or by actually having lived there for the greater part of a year.[27] For people with no fixed abode (*vagi*) the proper tribunal is the court of the diocese in which they are staying.[28] The tribunals of the domicile or quasi-domicile are equally competent but according to Maroto, the tribunal of domicile is to be preferred.[29]

As a safeguard against the danger that a quasi-domicile may have been obtained fraudulently for the purpose of escaping the court of domicile where the marriage was contracted and where the

[22] *Apollinaris,* I (1928), 303. Kay, *Competence in Matrimonial Procedure,* p. 88 sq.

[23] *Jus Pontificium,* VI (1926), 159; *Apollinaris,* I (1928), 304.

[24] Gasparri, *De Matrimonio,* n. 1463.

[25] Can. 1964.

[26] Can. 92, §1, §3.

[27] Can. 92, §2.

[28] Cans. 94, §2; 1563.

[29] Maroto, *Institutiones Juris Canonici* I, n. 415.

circumstances of the marriage and the persons are better known to the court, the Sacred Congregation of the Sacraments, December 23, 1929, issued an Instruction [30] relative to the steps to be taken by the judges and defender of the bond of the court of quasi-domicile before a case is admitted to court for the reason of quasi-domicile. The points outlined in the Instruction are as follows:

> I. Before the judge admits a case of nullity of marriage taken to his court for reason of quasi-domicile, he shall with the assistance of the Defender of the Bond consider the following points:
>
> (1) whether the title of quasi-domicile under which the case is to be tried by the court has been acquired in conformity with Canon Law;
>
> (2) whether the parties allege any reason, and what the reason is, why they want the case tried outside the court of domicile or the place of contract;
>
> (3) under what head they allege the nullity of the marriage;
>
> (4) what proofs and documents can be more easily produced in this court while the parties are far away from the place of domicile or the place of contract;
>
> (5) information is to be obtained about the truth of the petition and about the proofs from the Curias of the Ordinaries of domicile and place of contract. It shall not be lawful to proceed with the case until this information has been obtained and judged sufficient. If the Ordinary answers that the parties have sought to get a court for reason of quasi-domicile to make it difficult for the court to ascertain the truth, and that for this reason the Ordinary requests that the case be remanded to his court, the court of quasi-domicile shall thoroughly consider the question whether it is proper to assent to the request of the Ordinary.
>
> II. In this inquiry conducted before the case is accepted the Defender of the Bond shall according to Canons 1968, 1969 and 1984 do the following:
>
> (1) propose appropriate questions on the foregoing points;
>
> (2) study the answers of the parties or the documents exhibited, make objections, and request the court to examine some witnesses, or that other information be obtained, as the case may be.
>
> III. Though the Defender of the Bond is at liberty to object and to strive to prevent the evils that this Instruction intends

[30] S. C. de Sac. Instr. Dec. 23, 1929—*A.A.S.*, XXII (1930), 168 sq.

to prevent, nevertheless the judge to whom the case is brought by reason of quasi-domicile has the right to conduct this preliminary investigation and rule whatever seems fair to him in settling this point after the manner of incidental questions spoken of in Canons 1837-1841.

IV. (1) The judge shall have the parties summoned to court, and also the witnesses, at the instance of the parties, or of the Defender of the Bond (calling them *ex officio*), and have them questioned, using for this purpose the forms of questions submitted by the Defender according to the rules of law;

(2) the judge shall conduct the case in such a manner that there may not be too many witnesses or instruments, and documents which are not strictly to the point are to be excluded, as otherwise this question which is outside the regular trial and which should be settled by a short process, would become too complicated and would open the way to fraud and malice;

(3) wherefore, as soon as he thinks that sufficient proofs and arguments have been furnished, the judge may declare the question closed after having consulted the Defender of the Bond;

(4) after this, the judge shall consider the proofs advanced, the objections of the Defender of the Bond, the information received from the Ordinaries of the place of marriage and place of contract, and give the latter special consideration if these Ordinaries request that the case be remanded to them. Finally, he shall issue a decree by which he gives the case either to the court of the quasi-domicile or to that of the place of domicile or the place of contract;

(5) if the Defender of the Bond is not satisfied with the decision and requests that the case be remanded to either the place of domicile or of contract, he shall state in writing the reasons why he makes such a demand;

(6) the parties—either of them—are at liberty to object to the decree of the judge and to present written arguments or documents;

(7) after the judge has carefully considered the objections he is, in virtue of Canon 1841, at liberty to correct or revoke his decree;

(8) if the judge after due deliberation persists in his decree and confirms it, the incidental question shall, through recourse of the Defender of the Bond, be taken to the Sacred Congregation of the Sacraments.

V. (1) Whenever the question of the nullity of a marriage has been decided by the judge of the quasi-domicile, and the Sacred Congregation does not consider him competent, the Defender of the Bond of the court of appeal must first of all insist on the examination of the acts by which the competency of the judge of quasi-domicile was established, and if he believes the competency was not well established, he shall refer the matter to the Sacred Congregation;

(2) if a case of nullity of marriage was introduced in a court for reason of quasi-domicile before this present Instruction was published, the Defender of the Bond shall inquire into the question of competency and produce arguments and proofs. If he has serious suspicion that fraud, deceit or error concerning the competency have occurred, he shall refer the matter to the Sacred Congregation;

(3) the Defender of the Bond has the same right and duty in the third and further instances of a cause of nullity.

When both parties are Catholics, if the husband is defendant the proper tribunal is the domicile or quasi-domicile of the husband. If there is a multiplicity of forums, the choice of the forum belongs to the wife. Should the wife be defendant if she is living with her husband, the proper tribunal is that of the domicile of her husband [31] or the quasi-domicile of her husband.[32] If the defendant wife has legitimately separated from her husband,[33] the proper court is determined by the domicile or quasi-domicile of the wife. If the wife is illegitimately separated from her husband (this includes cases where the wife has been maliciously deserted) the proper tribunal is either the domicile of the husband [34] or the quasi-domicile of the wife.[35]

In causes where one of the parties is a non-Catholic, the proper tribunal is that of the Catholic party whether defendant or plaintiff.[36] This must be understood without prejudice to the tribunal of the place of contract. A Catholic woman illegitimately separated from her non-Catholic husband and who has a quasi-domicile of her own, can sue her husband either in the diocese of her quasi-domicile or in the diocese of the domicile of her husband.[37]

[31] Can. 93, §1.

[32] Can. 93, §1; Maroto, *o. c.*, I, 412-413; Chelodi, *Jus de Personis*, p. 166; Wernz-Vidal, II, n. 12.

[33] Cans. 1130, 1131, §1.

[34] Can. 93, §1.

[35] Can. 93, §2.

[36] Can. 1964.

[37] Pont. Com. Int. Cod., July 14, 1922, *A.A.S.*, XIV (1922), 529.

If there is a question of the validity of a marriage contracted between Catholics of different rites, when the plaintiff belongs to one rite, and the defendant to another, the tribunal of the Ordinary of the rite and domicile of the defendant is the proper tribunal.[38] If both plaintiff and defendant belong to the same rite the tribunal of that bishop is proper, to whom both parties belong by reason of domicile and quasi-domicile and rite.[39]

C. *Other Titles of Competence.* There are other ways of acquiring a forum besides those mentioned in Canon 1964 which may be applied to matrimonial causes. A visitor in Rome is privileged to accept citation before the tribunal of the diocese of Rome[40] and one who has been in Rome a year can refuse citation in the forum of his proper Ordinary and demand to be cited before the tribunal of the diocese of Rome.[41] A visitor in Rome with a domicile or quasi-domicile elsewhere can refuse citation before the tribunal of the diocese of Rome and demand that the cause be decided by his proper Ordinary if this request is made before the citation to appear before the diocesan tribunal of Rome is accepted.[42]

Spoliation. Because of danger of sin the *actio spolii* in regard to the restoration of the rights of cohabitation would scarcely be urged in matrimonial causes of nullity before the existence of the alleged invalidity is disproved.[43]

Prevenience. When two or more diocesan tribunals are equally competent to try a matrimonial cause, the right to decide the matter becomes proper to that tribunal by which the defendant was first legitimately cited.[44] Competence by reason of prevenience is only possible between equally competent tribunals. Prevenience in matrimonial causes of nullity is possible because the diocesan tribunal of the place of contract, domicile and quasi-domicile are equally competent, and hence optional.

[38] Can. 98, §4.
[39] Cappello, *De Matrimonio,* n. 868.
[40] Can. 1599, §2.
[41] Can. 1562, §2.
[42] Cans. 1562, §2, 1568, 1725.
[43] Lega, *De Judiciis Ecclesiasticis,* I, n. 231.
[44] Can. 1568.

Art. IV. Who Has the Right to Attack the Validity of a Marriage?

The following persons are capable of attacking a marriage in matrimonial causes of nullity:

1. The parties themselves unless they were the cause of the impediment. The word *impediment* in Canon 1917, §1, n. 1 is to be understood of diriment impediments properly so called [45] and also of those improperly so called [46] such as fear and force condition, etc.[47] The Pontifical Commission for the Authentic Interpretation of the Code declared on February 17, 1930, that those persons who are incapable of accusing a marriage by virtue of Canon 1971, §1, n. 1, have the right to denounce such a marriage to the Ordinary or the promoter of justice.[48] For example, a marriage cannot be attacked by the party who was the cause of error, or force or of the fact that the condition attached to the marriage was not fulfilled, but they can denounce such a marriage to the Ordinary or promoter of justice, and the latter will assume the function of plaintiff in the case. The innocent party has always the right to attack the marriage even though a long time has elapsed and after prolonged cohabitation. Consummation of the marriage in such cases establishes only a presumption in favor of the validity of the marriage, and this presumption does not exist if the legitimate form is necessary for the validation.

2. The promoter of justice has the right to attack a marriage invalid by virtue of any impediment public of its very nature.[49]

Canon 1037 defines an impediment to be public when it can be proved in court. Various interpretations have been given to this canon. Wernz-Vidal [50] regard any impediment as public by its nature if it arises out of a fact which must take place publicly such as an ordination or a religious profession; or out of facts of which there is a public record, like age, consanguinity, etc.; or if the facts can

[45] Cans. 1067-1080.

[46] Cans. 1081-1103.

[47] Pont. Com. Int. Cod., Mar. 12, 1929—*A.A.S.*, XXI (1929), 171.

[48] *A.A.S.*, XXII (1930), 196.

[49] Cans. 1037; 1971, §1, n. 2.

[50] *Jus Canonicum* V, n. 147.

be proved by the testimony of a qualified witness. Vermeersch-Cruesen [51] regard those impediments as public by nature which can be proved in court by witnesses or documents. Noval [52] holds that marriages invalid by reason of impediments which are occult by nature such as impotency, force and fear, etc.—after the presence of these impediments has actually become known to others in such a way that they can be proved in court—can be attacked by the promoter of justice.

The following have no right to attack a marriage.[53]

1. All other persons, even blood relatives, have no right to attack the validity of a marriage or petition for a declaration of nullity on a marriage.[54] Relatives in the present legislation [55] have only the right to denounce an invalid marriage to the Ordinary or to the promoter of justice.

A marriage not accused during the lifetime is after the death of one or both parties, presumed to be valid and against this presumption no proof is admitted except when this question arises incidentally for example in connection with the rights of inheritance or the care and maintenance of children.[56]

Art. V. Acceptance or Rejection of the Libellus

When the petition or the *libellus* has been properly made it becomes the duty of the tribunal after establishing its competency and the right of the plaintiff to sue, to examine thoroughly the contents of the petition in order to find out whether the alleged nullifying impediment or defect of form or consent rests upon a probably solid basis. The plaintiff may be questioned or anyone else present

[51] *Epitome*, III, n. 286.

[52] *De Processibus*, n. 850.

[53] Can. 1971, §1.

[54] This is different from the old legislation which permitted near relatives to seek a declaration of nullity in certain causes like consanguinity, affinity, public propriety, etc. Formerly every Catholic was permitted to seek a declaration on marriages invalid because of an impediment of public right provided that at the time of publication of the banns he did not remain silent without a just cause. Schmalzgrueber IV, 18, n. 13.

[55] Can. 1971, §2.

[56] Can. 1972.

having knowledge of the case. If the defender of the bond is present he should be heard. If it is found in this examination of the petition by the tribunal that the presence of the impediment cannot be proved, or that the plaintiff has only slight and insufficient proofs, the tribunal should reject it or advise that the petition be withdrawn. But if it is found that the accusation or petition rests on a probably solid basis it should be admitted. The acceptance or rejection of the petition can be passed on by the Official or by an auditor, or by the integral tribunal. If the entire tribunal passes on the acceptance, or rejection of the bill of complaint or *libellus,* the order of the business in the session might be as follows:

1. Reading of the appointment of the synodal or pro-synodal judges who with the Official are to hear the case.
2. The appointment of the *Ponens* for the case by the Official.
3. The reading of the appointment of the other officers of the court for the case—defender of the bond, notary, advocates, procurators, etc.
4. The reading of the petition of the plaintiff.
5. Objections of the defender of the bond.
6. Correction of bill if necessary, or the acceptance or rejection by the tribunal.
7. Appointment of advocates for the parties if they have not already been chosen.
8. Issuing of the decree of acceptance or rejection of the petition by the Official.

Usually the Official accepts or rejects the petition. The acceptance or the rejection of the bill of petition or accusation is made by a decree of the Official signed by him and the notary. A number should be given to the bill which should be used on every page of the acts thereafter. If the petition is rejected the reason for the refusal must be stated, whether refusal is based on contents of the bill, the incompetence of the tribunal or the incapability of the plaintiff to bring suit. If the rejection is because of formal defects in the bill itself, which can be amended, a new and corrected bill may be presented. If this corrected bill is rejected the reasons must be given for the new refusal.

Recourse may then be had by the plaintiff within ten days to the higher court (established court of appeal) against the rejection of the bill; and the tribunal of appeal, having heard the party, and the defender of the bond (or the promoter of justice) shall hand down a prompt ruling on the rejection. These ten days are *tempus utile* and recourse is not barred to the plaintiff if through ignorance or impossibility to act, he was unable to have recourse to the court of appeal within the proper time.[57]

If the tribunal to which the case was first presented makes no move either to accept or reject the bill, after the expiration of one month (*tempus continuum*) [58] from the date when the bill was presented, the plaintiff may insist that the tribunal act, and may invoke Canon 1625 in order to force action. If the tribunal is inactive for five days longer recourse should be had by the plaintiff to the Ordinary asking him to compel the tribunal to act, or if the Ordinary is presiding over the tribunal, recourse may be had to the higher court asking it to compel the Ordinary to act or to substitute another presiding judge to try the case.[59]

Art. VI. The Citation of the Defendant

After the decree of acceptance of the *libellus*, the next step is the citation of the defendant. The citation of the defendant is made by the Official. The citation may be written on the bill of complaint, or adjoined to it, so that the defendant may know immediately the nature of the case, and prepare his defense. Notification should at the same time be sent to the plaintiff, to appear on a specified day, and at a fixed hour before the tribunal, and informing him when copy of the defendant's answer may be had.[60] The names of the judges who are to try the case and the name of the defender of the bond are included in notice to the plaintiff. A summons is peremptory and need not be repeated unless the tribunal wishes to punish for contempt of court a party who ignores the first summons.[61] A summons is not necessary if both contending

[57] Cans. 1709, 35.

[58] Can. 35.

[59] Can. 1710.

[60] Can. 1712.

[61] Cans. 1714-1845, §2.

parties voluntarily appear before the tribunal to present their case, but the notary shall make note in the acts of the case that the parties came of their own accord.[62]

The summons shall be made clearly and distinctly in writing. It shall express a precept or command to the defendant to appear. It shall contain the name of the Official who issues it, the names of the other judges who with the Official, are to try the case, so that the parties may know immediately whether the tribunal is competent or not, and whether they wish to take exception of any kind against the judges of the tribunal. It shall indicate at least in general terms the reason why the party is summoned, give the correct name and surname of the plaintiff and defendant, the place where, and the date when (year, month, day, hour), he is to appear. It must be sealed with the seal of the tribunal and signed by the Official and the notary.[63] The summons should be made in duplicate, one to be delivered to the defendant and the other to be inserted in the acts of the case and preserved. Intimation of the summons may be made in three ways, by courier, registered mail or edict. If a courier is used, after he has found the party he must deliver the summons into his hands, sign the summons marking the date and hour of delivery. If the party refuses to accept the summons, the courier shall sign the summons, noting the day and the hour of refusal, and return it to the Official. A defendant who refuses to accept summons is considered as duly summoned. If the defendant is not at home, the courier may leave the summons with some person of the defendant's family, or with his servant, if they are willing to accept it, and promise to give it to the defendant as soon as he returns, otherwise, it shall be returned to the Official.[64] If he leaves the summons, he will sign as stated before, and add the name of the person to whom the summons was given. The courier shall make a written report of his work to the Official and sign it, and it shall be inserted in the acts.[65]

[62] Can. 1711.
[63] Can. 1723.
[64] Can. 1717.
[65] Can. 1722.

The method generally in use in the United States for summoning the parties is the mail service. But the letter must be registered, and a return receipt demanded, and the receipt must be inserted in the acts. The use of the registered letter is sanctioned by legitimate custom.[66]

The third method of summoning the parties is by edict or public notice. This may be done by attaching the summons to the door of the curia, or courtroom, for a period of time considered sufficient by the Official, or by publishing it in the diocesan bulletin or newspaper, or in the public press. A report of this service if it is used, is to be made in writing, and signed by the notary of the tribunal and added to the acts of the trial.

Once a judicial citation has been made, a change of domicile on the part of the spouses, does not modify the competence of the tribunal which first issued the summons.

If the summons of the defendant was properly made and he neither appears personally, or by proxy, and he gives no just excuse for absenting himself, he is to be declared contumacious and the trial is to proceed in his absence.[67] This declaration of contumacy may be made upon the demand of the other party or of the promoter of justice or of the defender of the bond. If it is not certain that the summons reached the defendant, a second summons should be issued and a term assigned for the defendant's appearance, and only after that time has expired may contumacy be declared. Ecclesiastical penalties can be used to force a contumacious person, only after it has been proved, that a second summons was ineffective, or unheeded, and provided the threat of these penalties was directly mentioned in the second summons.[68]

After the citation of the defendant, exceptions are in order. The defendant either personally or through his advocate or procurator may take exception to the capacity of the plaintiff, to the form of the petition, to the facts alleged in the petition, to the competency of the court, or to the person of the judges, the defender of the bond or other officers of the court. These exceptions must be pro-

[66] Can. 1719.
[67] Can. 1729.
[68] Can. 1845.

posed and disposed of before the *litis contestatio*, and are admissible after that time, only if the party declares under oath that they become known to him after the *litis contestatio*.[69] However the exception of the absolute incompetency of the judge may be proposed at any time during the trial.[70] The exception of excommunication against either the plaintiff or the judges may also be brought up at any time during the trial.

The effects of legitimate citation in matrimonial causes are: the person cited is bound to appear in court unless he has a just excuse; the case is considered pending, hence the status of the person cannot be changed; competency of the judge is established; the person cited obtains the right of standing in court even though in reality he has no such right, and the jurisdiction of the judge is continued, i.e., the party cited is obliged to appear before the judge even though he has become subject to another Ordinary.

[69] Can. 1628, §1.
[70] Can. 1628, §2.

CHAPTER VIII

THE TRIAL PROPER

AFTER the plaintiff as well as the defendant have explained their version of the facts of the case, and clearly fixed the issue, the next step is, that the plaintiff shall prove his statements and the defendant and the defender of the bond shall attempt to disprove or refute them. In other words the plaintiff shall now produce before the tribunal his witnesses, experts, documents, etc., to show that the alleged impediment or defect really exists. Afterward the defendant and the defender of the bond produce witnesses, experts, documents, etc., for the purpose of overthrowing the proofs brought forward by the plaintiff and of demonstrating that the alleged impediment does not exist in the case. This present stage of the trial, the production of proof, comprises the examination of 1. the parties; 2. witnesses; 3. experts; 4. documents.

ART. I. SOME GENERAL RULES

In matrimonial causes the oath to tell the truth must be demanded of both parties, whether they appear personally to be examined before the tribunal, or if legitimately excused from appearing and are examined elsewhere by an auditor or delegate of the tribunal.[1] Every witness with the exception of unfit and suspected witnesses [2] before testifying must take the oath that they will state the truth, the whole truth and nothing but the truth. The tribunal may likewise require of a witness on the conclusion of his examination an oath on the truth of the statements made during the examination.[3] Witnesses may likewise be required to take an oath of secrecy with reference to the questions proposed to them, and the answers given by them, until the acts and proofs are made public; or they may

[1] Cans. 1744, 1770, §2, n. 2.

[2] Can. 1758.

[3] Can. 1768.

even be bound to perpetual secrecy, if the testimony is of such a nature that defamation, discord or other grave evils are feared from its publication.[4] This same oath may be demanded of the parties, their advocates and procurators and the experts.[5] Experts are required to take an oath to fulfill their duties faithfully.[6]

Before administering the oath to these persons, the Official or the one examining them will admonish them of the sanctity of their oath, of the gravity of the sin of perjury, and of the penalties which may be inflicted upon those who swear falsely.[7]

A. *Tenor of Questions.* The questions to be proposed are partly general, and partly special.

Of a general character are the preliminary questions of name and surname, parentage, age, religion, condition, profession, residence and also their connection with the parties in the case.

The special questions will touch upon the merits of the case, i.e., on the matrimonial cause which is being disputed. They shall be questioned concerning the impediment which it is alleged renders the marriage invalid and all the circumstances connected with it. The questions therefore will in each case rest on the nature of the particular impediment.

It is impossible and inadvisable to attempt anything like a standard form of interrogatory. The interrogatory should be drawn up in accordance with the allegations in the case and the points of law involved. For example, in a case of force and fear (*vis et metus*)[8] the interrogatories should concern the circumstances that resulted in the marriage, the nature and disposition of the man or woman in question, of the parents, of the presumed authors of the force and fear; the nature of the coercion, the motives on account of which the coerced party refused this marriage, particularly, whether he or she had in view marriage with another; the motives that inspired those who caused the coercion. The interrogatories should likewise concern the means of force employed, violence,

[4] Cans. 1623, §3, 1769.
[5] Can. 1623, §3.
[6] Can. 1797, §1.
[7] Can. 1743, §3.
[8] Can. 1083.

threats, pleadings. They should be questioned too about the resistance of the coerced party, whether a third party intervened, whether it continued from the beginning up to the marriage, and after the marriage, whether the marriage was consummated, what the reasons were for the separation, why the coerced person did not protest sooner. Similar points of interrogation with congruous changes may be prepared for other defects and impediments. The questioning of witnesses will follow along the same line, with the purpose of giving the tribunal information worthy of belief on the points under discussion, and of convincing it of the truth or untruth of the answers given by the parties, and thus helping it to arrive at moral certainty with regard to the case.

The person questioned shall likewise be asked from what source and how he obtained the knowledge of the things he asserts.[9] Those questioned should be examined in as quick a succession as possible, that is, within as short an interval as possible, in order that the case may be expedited, and conversations between the witnesses and parties hindered, and collusion prevented. All questions are asked by the Official or his delegate.[10] The questions must be brief, simple, not complicated or captious or cunning, or in any manner offensive, nor irrelevant to the case in question. The Official ordinarily rules on the propriety of questions. He may likewise change them.[11]

All those questioned shall answer orally. The answers are committed to writing word for word by the notary, and before the person questioned leaves the stand, his testimony must be read to him, and he must be given leave to add, suppress, correct or vary his statements.[12] The Official or auditor and the person examined and notary must sign the document.[13]

In recording the minutes of the examination the notary shall state whether the oath was taken or refused, record the names of all those present, whether other questions than those proposed orig-

[9] Can. 1774.

[10] Can. 1773, §2.

[11] *Regulae Servandae*, S.R.R. §140.

[12] Can. 1777.

[13] Can. 1780, §2.

inally by the other party, and the defender of the bond, were asked during the examination, and generally everything that is worth putting on record, that happened during the hearing should be put down in writing.[14]

Art. II. Joining of Issues and the Examination of the Parties

Ordinarily there is no formal joining of issues (*litis contestatio*) in matrimonial causes. This is supplied by the examination of the parties. It suffices that they appear before the Official or the auditor and from questions and answers given during the examination, clarify the issue. The bill of complaint and the reply thereto of the defendant [15] will indicate in the course of the examination the point or points to be decided by the court. If the defendant fails to appear, the tribunal formulates the issue.[16] The *dubium concordandum* customarily reads as follows:

> *An constet de nullitate matrimonii inter . . . et . . . capite (e.g. vis et metus)?*

This then, if established by the examination of the parties, will serve as the issue to be submitted to the discussion and decision of the tribunal. The points at issue usually receive documentation in the filing of the petition of the plaintiff and reply of the defendant. In matrimonial causes the presiding judge or the auditor puts the issue on the record by stating it in the form of a decree.[17]

The parties shall be duly summoned, or notified by the Official to appear before the tribunal or its auditor on an appointed day and at a specified hour. The defender of the bond shall likewise be cited. Each party must be examined separately and before the examination begins an oath to tell the truth must be demanded of each party.[18] Those who may be present at this examination are

[14] Can. 1779.
[15] Can. 1727.
[16] Can. 1729, §1.
[17] Can. 1729, §2, §3.
[18] Can. 1744.

the judges of the tribunal, or an auditor, the notary, the defender of the bond, the procurators and the advocates of the parties. The Official proposes the questions submitted to him by the plaintiff, the defendant, the defender of the bond and any that he himself or the other judges wish to ask.[19] The notary sets down in writing both the questions and answers. The oath must be taken and the questions responded to personally by the parties.[20] If either party is detained from appearing personally before the tribunal by sickness or any other physical or mental impediment, they may be questioned at their respective residence and the tribunal may send an auditor and notary to receive the deposition. The questioning shall include the interrogatories of the other party, of the defender of the bond and whatever questions the auditor may think it expedient to add.[21] If either party dwells outside the diocese, and cannot conveniently return and appear in court, their deposition according to Canon 1570, §2, must be received by their local tribunal, in accordance with the formulary of interrogation and the instructions sent to it by the tribunal hearing the case. The deposition of a party who lives so far away from the court that it would be expensive for them to come to court or for the judge to reach them may be taken by a worthy and fit priest who lives near the place. The interrogatories must be forwarded to the priest by the tribunal and he must have with him another person who is to act as notary.[22] The oath shall precede and conclude the questioning in every case.

The plaintiff is questioned first, for the burden of proof falls upon him who accuses the marriage, whether he is one of the married couple, or the promoter of justice. The plaintiff will in court, and under oath affirm the invalidity of the marriage, and then fully and with all necessary details, repeat what he has stated in the written petition for a declaration of nullity, and also in the extrajudicial preliminary investigation, and he shall answer whatever questions are proposed by the Official.

Next the defendant is questioned, that is, one of the spouses if

[19] Can. 1745.

[20] Can. 1746.

[21] Can. 1770, §2, n. 2.

[22] Can. 1770, §4.

one is plaintiff, or both spouses if the marriage is attacked by a third party. They will under oath give their version of the alleged impediment, denying in whole or in part the allegations of the plaintiff and give answer to all other questions legitimately proposed to them.

In matrimonial causes in which the validity of a marriage is in question, a judicial confession against the validity of a marriage, whether oral or written, by one party against himself and in favor of another, or by both parties, whether made spontaneously or at the demand of the tribunal, is not sufficient and has in itself no proof value, because the public welfare is concerned.[23] The same can be said of extrajudicial confessions of the parties. The reason is very clear.

Contumacy of the parties in refusing to appear for trial or any similar act cannot be taken as a presumption against their marriage.

Art. III. The Examination of Witnesses

Witnesses may be produced by the plaintiff, the defendant, the defender of the bond and the tribunal *ex officio*. Citation is made by the Official or the auditor after the names of the witnesses are presented to the court. Citation shall be sent to each witness, stating the place of the hearing, the day, month, year and hour. It shall be signed by the Official or the auditor and by the notary.[24] Citation may be made in the same way in which the parties are summoned. The questions upon which the witnesses are to be examined should be handed to the tribunal before the time set for the examination. If this has not been done on the day set by the tribunal, it is considered that the party has withdrawn his request for summoning the witness or witnesses. The tribunal may admit as many witnesses as are necessary to bring out the truth.[25] In certain cases, for example, impotency, if the facts are not ascertained from other sources the Code requires each of the parties to produce witnesses (*septimae manus*), related to the parties by blood or affinity,

[23] Can. 1751.
[24] Can. 1765.
[25] Can. 1754.

or at least neighbors of good reputation, or otherwise well informed persons, who will testify under oath to the credibility and veracity of the parties alleging impotence and in particular to their veracity on the point. Their testimony adds weight to the deposition of the parties but it is not complete proof; it must be supported by other arguments or circumstances.[26]

Witnesses legitimately questioned must answer and tell the truth, and those not exempted by law may be forced to testify under penalty of exclusion from all ecclesiastical acts,[27] for a time to be determined by the judge according to the circumstances of the case. In case of the inability of the witness to appear, the tribunal should be informed of the reason. Provision may be made for the examination of witnesses who cannot appear or who live at a distance or outside the territory of the tribunal as is done for the examination of the parties in similar circumstances.[28]

Witnesses who refuse to testify or who having testified are detected in a lie are punished by exclusion from the legitimate ecclesiastical acts for a time to be determined by the Judge. If the witnesses have taken an oath to tell the truth and are detected in a lie the penalty is more severe, a layman is punished by a personal interdict and a cleric is suspended.[29] Anyone who presumes to induce a witness or an expert by promises or in any other manner to give false testimony or conceal the truth incurs the same penalties as those who violate their oath or conceal the truth.[30]

A. *Certain Persons Disqualified from Acting as Witnesses.* The parties in a case, the persons who take the place of the parties, the judges and those who assist the judges, and advocates and others who assist or have assisted the parties in the case are disqualified from acting as witnesses. Priests are to be rejected as witnesses in whatever concerns knowledge gained through sacramental confession, even though by the will of the penitent they had been freed from the seal of confession. Whatever has been heard by anyone in any

[26] Can. 1975.
[27] Can. 2256.
[28] Cfr. p. 110.
[29] Can. 1743.
[30] Cans. 1755, §3, 1743, 2256.

manner on the occasion of a confession cannot be accepted even as an indication of the truth. Ordinarily blood relatives and relatives by marriage in every degree in the direct line and in the first degree of the collateral line would be declared incapable of being witnesses, but they are permitted to testify in marriage cases.[31]

The Code considers children under the age of puberty (boys 14 years and girls 12 years of age) and weakminded persons as unfit witnesses.[32] In the class of weakminded persons are included idiots, mentally deranged persons, and persons under the influence of drugs or intoxicating liquor. Those who are defective in speech, sight or hearing are not to be excluded provided those defects were not present at the time the act occurred with regard to which they are to testify.

The following witnesses are to be rejected as suspected: 1. All excommunicated and infamous persons after a condemnatory or declaratory sentence; 2. Persons whose character is such as to render their testimony untrustworthy; 3. Persons who have publicly fostered enmity and hatred against the party against whom they are called to testify.[33]

The tribunal may and should admit as witnesses in matrimonial causes all who are not absolutely incompetent but their testimony constitutes at most indications or clues for further inquiries, not proofs.[34]

A party may renounce the privilege of examining a witness but the opponent may demand despite this renunciation that the witness be examined.[35] If a witness not legitimately cited, voluntarily appears, the tribunal may admit or reject him since there is reason to suspect the motives of such a witness, and he must be rejected if it becomes apparent that the motive of such a witness is simply to delay the trial or obstruct justice and truth.[36] The tribunal or its auditor must *ex officio* exclude incapable, unfit and suspected witnesses un-

[31] Cans. 1757-1974.
[32] Can. 1757, §1.
[33] Can. 1757, §2.
[34] Wernz-Vidal, *Jus Canonicum* V, n. 700.
[35] Can. 1759.
[36] Can. 1760.

less they are admitted to give presumptive evidence.[37] A party may take exception to witnesses unless he has introduced them. The producing party must show that the reason for the exception developed since he proposed the witness, if he wishes to take exception to a witness that he himself proposed. Objections to witnesses should be made within three days from the time the names are made known to the other party. Unless a presumption of law stands against a witness, or his defect is notorious, or the reason for the objection can be immediately and easily proved, or could not be proved later on, discussions on exceptions against witnesses should be postponed until the end of the examination of the witnesses but should be heard before the publication of the testimony.[38] If exceptions are sustained, this should be done by a decree of the Official, signed by him and the notary, stating the reasons for the rejection.

Ordinarily only the tribunal, or its auditor, the defender of the bond, the notary, the procurators and the advocates may be present at the examination of a witness. The Official or the auditor puts all questions to the witness, even those which arise during the examination. After the general questions the Official may propose the questions prepared by the parties, then the questions of the defender of the bond and any other questions the tribunal *ex officio* may wish to propose.

Each witness is examined separately. Before testifying all witnesses except the unfit and suspected must swear they will tell the truth, the whole truth and nothing but the truth.[39] The parties may be present at the taking of the oath, unless the judge does not think it advisable to let the parties know who the witnesses are.[40] Witnesses may at the discretion of the tribunal be confronted with one another and with the parties, only, if they disagree among themselves or with the party for whom they testify on a serious or substantial point, and if in the opinion of the judges, there is no better or easier way to discover the truth, and if there is no danger of

[37] Cans. 1765-1758.

[38] Can. 1766; Noval, n. 479.

[39] Can. 1758.

[40] Cans. 1767, §2, 1758.

scandal or discord arising from the confronting of these various persons.[41]

In regard to the character of questions to be submitted to the witnesses, what was said in a previous chapter in regard to the questions to be used at the examination of parties, applies here. The witness should answer the questions put to him and therefore he should not go outside or beyond them or volunteer testimony. The answers should be clear, determined, not vacillating, and free from contradictions. Canon 1761, §1, states that the questions on which a witness is to be cross-examined must not be communicated to him before hand, i. e., before he has been sworn and placed on the stand. Answers given by witnesses are to be made orally[43] and are to be immediately reduced verbatim to writing by the notary.[44] At the conclusion of the testimony, it is to be read to the witness and he may add, suppress, correct, or change any statement he has made. After the reading of the testimony and the statement of the witness that it is correct, the tribunal or the auditor may require the witness to take an oath as to the correctness of the testimony.[45] Then the witness, the Official or the one who takes his place and the notary sign the document.[46]

In the minutes of the examination the notary must state whether the oaths were taken, refused by, or remitted to the witness, whether other questions than those originally proposed were asked *ex officio,* and generally everything that is worth putting on the record that happened during the examination of the witness.[47]

A witness may be examined repeatedly before the publication of the testimony at the request of the parties, or if the tribunal deems it necessary or useful.[48]

Immediately after the examination of the witness the testimony may be published, or the tribunal may defer the publication until all

[41] Can. 1772, §1, §2, §3.

[43] Can. 1777.

[44] Can. 1778.

[45] Can. 1768.

[46] Can. 1780, §2.

[47] Can. 1779.

[48] Cans. 1762, 1781.

proof material has been gathered. Exceptions may be made to the depositions of witnesses either, because the examination was not conducted legally, or because of alleged falsehoods, contradictions, etc. If these exceptions are admitted the tribunal shall set a term for proving them.

Art. IV. Testimony of Experts

The services of experts are frequently needed in matrimonial causes, for example, in cases of impotency, or cases wherein defective consent is based on insanity; likewise in cases where it is necessary to determine the authenticity of writings or documents. In Canon Law experts (*periti*) are witnesses of definite qualifications who on account of their special knowledge, or on account of their special experience are able to discover specific facts about a case, to estimate these facts and to prove them. They are chosen by the Official in consultation with the defender of the bond or promoter of justice.[49] Those should be chosen as experts who hold a certificate or diploma as to their fitness from competent public authority.[50] Before entering upon their office they must take an oath to faithfully fulfill their office.[51] Experts may be excluded for the same reasons as witnesses are excluded.[52] Exceptions may be taken against them.[53]

The tribunal should define as nearly and clearly as possible the exact purpose for which the aid of the expert is asked, taking into consideration the suggestions of the parties. The litigant parties may be present when the experts perform their duties unless the law forbids or the delicacy of the matter in question makes their presence undesirable. A term should be set within which time the report of the experts should be made.[54] These experts are to be questioned separately by the tribunal on points previously drawn up by the defender of the bond, and they must answer under oath.

[49] Can. 1793.
[50] Can. 1795, §1.
[51] Can. 1797.
[52] Can. 1795, §2.
[53] Can. 1796.
[54] Can. 1799.

In cases of impotence or non-consummation those who have previously examined the parties concerning the point upon which the petition for a declaration of nullity is based are not to be admitted as experts [55] but they may be admitted as witnesses. Experts in cases where lack of consent for reasons of insanity is alleged, should be different from those who formerly visited the patient, but this latter class must be heard as witnesses.[56] In cases of impotence, women have the choice of physicians or of legally approved midwives as experts and the examination is to be made in the presence of a worthy matron.[57] Experts may give their opinion in writing or orally in the presence of the tribunal or auditor and the notary. If their testimony is given orally it is reduced to writing by the notary. An expert if he gives his opinion in writing may be summoned by the tribunal to give whatever additional explanation seems necessary. Whether they give their testimony orally or in writing they shall indicate the ways and means adopted by them in carrying out the orders of the court and the reasons upon which their opinion is based.[58] In cases of divergent expert opinion other experts are to be called.[59] If several experts testify they must make up and sign individual reports.[60] The tribunal is not bound to accept an expert's opinion, but if it does, it should explain in a decree why it admitted or rejected their conclusions.

Art. V. Documents

Canon 1812 decrees that both public and private documents may be admitted in all kinds of trials. Letters and documents are often of great importance and interest in matrimonial causes. A public document is one composed by an official in his official capacity with due observance of the prescribed formalities of law.[61] A private

[55] Can. 1978.
[56] Can. 1982.
[57] Can. 1979.
[58] Can. 1801.
[59] Can. 1802.
[60] Can. 1980, §1.
[61] Santi-Leitner, II, 20, n. 2.

document is any writing executed by a private person, or by an official acting in his private capacity.[62] For a document to serve as evidence, it must be first determined whether it is genuine or authentic. Public documents are generally recognized by the name and title of the official issuing them, as well as his official seal or signature, the date and place of issuance. If a document bears the external marks of authenticity, its genuineness is generally presumed until called into question. The genuineness of a document may ordinarily be proved by the testimony of those who have signed it, or if this cannot be had by a comparison with other documents, or if necessary by the opinion of experts. Public ecclesiastical documents include acts confected by the Pope, the Roman Curia, and Ordinaries in authentic form, while in the exercise of their work, as well as authentic attestations of these same acts given by these officials or their notaries; instruments executed by ecclesiastical notaries; ecclesiastical judicial acts; inscriptions of baptism, confirmation, ordination, religious profession, marriage, and death, which are kept in the registers of a Curia, parish, or religious institute, and written attestations drawn from these records and confected by the parish priest, Ordinary, or ecclesiastical notary, or authentic copies of them.[63] Public civil documents are judged according to the common usage of the country.[64] These would include birth certificates, marriage licenses and records, certificates of death, burial permits, judicial acts and sworn statements witnessed by a notary or public official.

Private documents may be sources for establishing facts. Private writings [65] which the public law recognized directly or indirectly as true have a standing in judicial matters.[66] Authentic private documents,[67] will generally be signed writings drawn up with some

[62] Can. 1813, §3.

[63] Can. 1813, §1. Cfr. Lega, *De Iudiciis Ecclesiasticis,* I, n. 515.

[64] Can. 1813, §2.

[65] Can. 1813, §3.

[66] Cfr. can. 1817. Lega, *De Iudiciis Ecclesiasticis,* I, n. 515.

[67] Cfr. Bouix, *De Iudiciis Ecclesiasticis,* I, p. 322; Bassibey, *Le Mariage,* p. 349.

regard for form, such as a will. These are practically akin to public documents.[68] Private documents not recognized by public authority do not constitute approved proofs but lend a proof which must be substantiated (*probatio probanda*).[69] The value of these documents is restricted. If they are acknowledged by the party or recognized by the judge, they furnish proof *against* the author of them or the subscriber, or such persons as receive benefits from them.[70] Such writings are considered as an extrajudicial confession [71] but of themselves they have no proving force against any other persons than the three classes mentioned above.[72] There does not seem to be the insistence on the division of private documents into signed and unsigned [73] as formerly.[74] However, an unsigned document would not have much legal value.[75]

Documents have the force of legal proof only if deposited with the court either in the original or in an authenticated copy unless they have been published and are public property.[76] They may be attacked by the defender of the bond, by the parties, and rejected by the tribunal. The tribunal if it doubts the authenticity or correctness of a document may demand that the original be exhibited, or if this is impossible or inexpedient, it may delegate an auditor, or ask the local Ordinary to have the document examined and compared with the copy presented to the tribunal.[77]

An action may be instituted to compel the parties to exhibit documents in court, and the tribunal is competent to decide whether, and how, the exhibition is to be made, and in case the parties refuse

[68] Cfr. can. 1813, §2. Cf. can. 779, 1019, §2.

[69] Cfr. Lega, *De Iudiciis Ecclesiasticis,* I, n. 513; Bouix, *De Iudiciis Ecclesiasticis,* I, p. 323.

[70] E. g. the record of the birth of parents may enter in the matrimonial case of their children in respect to the impediment of consanguinity.

[71] Can. 1753.

[72] Can. 1817.

[73] Cfr. "*. . . adversus auctorem vel subscriptorem . . .*"—canon 1817.

[74] Cfr. Lega, *De Iudiciis Ecclesiasticis,* I, n. 516.

[75] Cfr. Kay, *Competence in Matrimonial Procedure,* p. 144 sq.

[76] Can. 1820.

[77] Can. 1821.

to exhibit certain documents, the tribunal shall decide what importance is to be attached to the refusal.[78]

Art. VI. Publication of the Process—Closing of the Evidence

After the plaintiff, and defendant, and the defender of the bond, have produced their witnesses, experts, documents, and other proofs, the entire proceedings are manifested to both parties. This is known as the publication of the process. This may be done in two ways. The parties and their advocates may inspect the acts of the process thus far conducted, or a copy of the acts may be given to them. The publication of the process will include minutes of the entire proceedings, the rulings of the tribunal, all the evidence submitted on both sides, the names and depositions of the witnesses, documents, papers, opinions, of experts. The Official through the notary or secretary of the tribunal will notify the parties, or their advocates, that the process has been published, and acquaint them of their right to inspect these acts and to present any further proofs they may have, or any objections they may have against the admissibility of the evidence or against the procedure as outlined in the acts. A term will be set by the tribunal [79] for the production of these objections.

The closing of the evidence (*conclusio in causa*) is declared by the Official or the auditor in a decree. This may be brought about in three ways: 1. The time for production of the evidence may have expired; 2. The parties may either voluntarily or at the request of the tribunal declare that they rest or have no further evidence to offer, or 3. The tribunal may declare itself sufficiently informed.[80] The defender of the bond should also be heard. The decree is issued and signed by the Official or the auditor and the notary.

Ordinarily in trials no new witnesses are admitted after the closing of the evidence (*conclusio in causa*), but in matrimonial causes the legislator permits the parties to bring new witnesses and new proof material after the *conclusio in causa*, provided no fraud or

[78] Can. 1824, §1, §2.
[79] Cans. 1858-1859.
[80] Can. 1860, §2.

bribe is employed, and provided both parties consent, and the defender does not object.[81] Witnesses may likewise be questioned again on the same points, provided the tribunal deems it necessary, and there is no danger of a secret agreement or bribery. The defender of the bond has always the right to object to the re-introduction of the same witness.[82]

Art. VII. Defense or Discussion of the Cause

After the case is closed (*conclusio in causa*) the tribunal shall fix a time for the defense.[83] The time may be prolonged at the request of one party, provided the other party is given a hearing on the postponement, and it may be shortened with the consent of both parties.[84] The defense is to be made in writing, and it may be printed only with the permission of the Official, and after he has examined the manuscripts. Five copies should be made of the defense writings, one for each judge, one for the defender of the bond and the parties must exchange their defense. The Official shall so direct the defense that it is not unduly prolonged, unless this matter is regulated by special laws of the tribunal.[85]

The purpose of the defense writings is to show how the proofs produced during the trial, viewed in the light of Canon Law, prove or disprove the validity, or invalidity of the marriage. In preparing the defense, it is the duty of the party or his advocate, to show what significance, weight and bearing the law of the Church gives to the individual proofs produced during the trial now being reviewed, and how each proof possesses the legal requisites or is destitute of them. It will be necessary for the advocates to go over carefully the entire evidence submitted on both sides, weigh each bit of evidence, note every point of advantage to his client and of disadvantage to the opponent and endeavor to bring the law of the Church to bear out and support his arguments, reasonings and de-

[81] Can. 1983.
[82] Cans. 1781-1983, §2.
[83] Can. 1862, §1.
[84] Can. 1862, §2.
[85] Can. 1864.

ductions. To do this intelligently, the advocate should divide his defense into different distinct heads corresponding to the different salient points of the controversy. Under each head he should group and enumerate those proofs produced in support of each point and show how these proofs fully and canonically prove the point. He should also under each head review the evidence produced by the other party or the defender of the bond concerning it, and show that it has not weakened or overthrown his party's position.

This may be illustrated with the same example of force and fear (*vis et metus*).[86] The advocate to make out his case should divide the defense into the following heads, viz.: 1. violence was really done, threats and whipping were suffered by the spouse and these threats and punishment caused fear; 2. these acts of violence were of a grave character and consequently the fear produced by them was serious; 3. this violence and the fear produced by it was unjust; 4. the acts of violence were inflicted by an external agent; 5. to free himself from which his client was compelled to choose marriage. The advocate will then discuss each of these points separately and under each of them he should review the proofs of every kind, adduced during the trial and bearing on the particular point, and show how these proofs thus properly grouped, demonstrate fully and canonically the respective point under which they are grouped.

The plaintiff or his advocate should arrange his defense first, and his writings are then communicated to the defendant or to his advocate to enable them to reply. This is usually done through the Official, who orders a copy of the plaintiff's defense sent to the defendant. The defendant or his advocate and the defender of the bond [87] in the case should divide their defense under the following heads: 1. there was really no fear or violence inflicted; 2. if there was fear or violence, it was light or trivial and not grave; 3. if there were acts of violence and they were of grave character, they were justly inflicted; 4. they were not inflicted for the purpose of inducing the party to consent to marriage but for some other reason; 5. the plaintiff has condoned the violence either expressly or tacitly and has thus ratified the marriage. The advocate will then discuss these points

[86] Can. 1087.

[87] Can. 1087.

separately, and show how the proofs produced during the trial both by the plaintiff and the defendant demonstrate their correctness and truth.

The defense of both parties will then be communicated to the defender of the bond for his objections. He should file his answer without unnecessary delay. A copy of this is delivered to the litigants who may answer it if they so desire. If they do reply, the defender of the bond always has the last word, and only after he has notified the tribunal that he has nothing further to say may it proceed to the sentence. Both parties must be given equal opportunity for defense.[88]

A brief oral discussion at the request of one or both parties may be permitted after the written defense, if the tribunal thinks it necessary to throw light on the subject. It must be made before the tribunal or its auditor, and a notary. The points to be discussed shall be briefly stated in writing and submitted to the tribunal. The Official shall communicate these points to both parties and shall set a date (day and hour) for the discussion of them. The defender of the bond shall be notified and may be present. If he is not present the minutes of the discussion shall be sent to him for his observations. The Official shall preside and the notary shall take down the minutes of the discussion, the admissions and conclusions arrived at, as often as the Official commands or either party with the consent of the Official demands it.[89]

Art. VIII. The Value or Weight of Proofs in Matrimonial Causes of Nullity

This article is merely an application of the general principles of proof contained in the Code to proofs offered in matrimonial causes.

A. *Witnesses*. The attention of the reader is called to what has already been said in a previous chapter regarding witnesses.[90]

The sworn statement of two, or three direct, unobjectionable, concordant witnesses, fully prove the existence of an alleged impedi-

[88] Can. 1865.
[89] Cans. 1866-1867.
[90] Cfr. p. 111.

ment and the subsequent invalidity of a marriage unless such testimony is weakened or contradicted by other witnesses equally worthy of belief or by circumstances which create a grave presumption.[91] They must be beyond suspicion and exception. Hence a certificate of a parish priest, or two other trustworthy persons attesting the probity and trustworthiness of the witnesses, is usually demanded in court. They must agree on the same point, for if one testified to one fact, and the other to another fact, they are not concordant but differing witnesses. The testimony of one witness, even though perfectly reliable, is not sufficient to establish the invalidity of a marriage, unless he is a qualified witness who makes a deposition concerning acts which he himself performed *ex officio*.[92]

B. *Experts and Ocular Inspection.* In cases of impotence, insanity, etc., the Code prescribes the hearing of experts. Two experts are required to constitute full proof, hence one alone is not sufficient as he may be deceived or he may be biased. The testimony of the two experts must be clear, concordant, and on and about the same fact, otherwise it proves nothing.

C. *Instruments and Documents.* Judicial proceedings of ecclesiastical courts are considered as public documents, hence the minutes and acts, documents and depositions of witnesses, of former judicial proceedings so far as they bear on the alleged defect or impediment, are considered as public documents if attested to by the notary of the court.

The presumption of law is in favor of public documents until the presumption is overthrown by evident arguments to the contrary. The burden of proof rests on the one attacking them.[93]

Private documents acknowledged as genuine by the party, or accepted as such by the judge, have the weight or value of an extrajudicial confession against the writer or those who derive their claim from him. These have no proving force against outsiders. This holds of course only for instruments that are produced in court, in the presence of the opponent and not contradicted by the opponent. Burden of proof is on the one asserting it is genuine.

[91] Can. 1791, §2

[92] Can. 1791, §1.

[93] Can. 1814.

Instruments that are lost by accident are proved by two witnesses worthy of belief who were present when it was written and know what it contained or in default of such witnesses by others who saw and read it afterwards. If an instrument was lost through the fault of one who alleges the loss he must prove the tenor of the instrument, the absence of fraud in the loss, and that it was not lost culpably. If an instrument was lost through the fault of an opponent, the person who affirms the loss is bound simply to affirm the iniquitous act of the opponent, and after this the contents are proved by the sole oath of the one from whom it is taken.[94]

D. *Witnesses Septimae Manus.* These witnesses are used in cases of impotence and non-consummation when the facts are not proved with certainty from other sources. These must be produced by both parties. They are taken from the blood relatives or relatives by marriage of each party, or if such cannot be had, from neighbors of good repute, or others who are well acquainted with the parties and who can testify to the probity of the parties and especially to their veracity concerning the matter in controversy.[95]

While the Code borrows the term *septimae manus* from the Decretal laws it does not specify the exact number of these auxiliary witnesses. In the examination they are to be treated as other witnesses, that is sworn in, etc., and they may be questioned by the tribunal and the defender of the bond. They testify to the probity of the party who produces them. Generally the deposition of the producing party is read to them and they are questioned on the veracity of the statements made by that party.[96] If in answering the questions legitimately proposed to them, they speak of anything directly touching the merits of the case itself, they should be asked from what source they obtained knowledge of the things they assert and how they obtained it.[97] Their testimony does not constitute full proof, because they do not testify about the facts of the case but rather

[94] Smith, *Marriage Process,* n. 584-586.

[95] Can. 1975.

[96] Inst. S. C. de Sac. Reg. 67, May 7, 1923, *A.A.S.,* XV (1923), 389.

[97] Can. 1774, §2.

about the character of the parties. They furnish additional strength to the deposition of the parties.

E. *Value of Proofs. Proofs which give a judge true moral certainty are:* (1) the testimony of two unexceptionable witnesses on the same point;[98] (2) a public or ecclesiastical document until disproved;[99] (3) the presumption of law;[100] (4) notoriety of fact or of law;[101] (5) facts asserted by one of the contending parties and admitted by the other unless the law or the judge demands proof;[102] (6) testimony of a qualified witness whose deposition concerns acts which he himself performed *ex officio*.[103]

Imperfect proofs or proofs which give probability but not moral certainty are: (1) Confession of the parties;[104] (2) testimony of one witness[105] or of two witnesses testifying to different points[106] or two witnesses who testify to the same point, but are suspected;[107] (3) writings of private character;[108] (4) presumptions not of law.[109]

F. *Presumptions.* A presumption is a reasonable conjecture or inference based upon a fact which is not perceived from another fact which is known with certainty.[110]

Presumptions are legal, and non legal or *ab homine*. Legal are *juris et de jure*, or *de jure tantum*.[111]

Simple legal presumptions hold a thing to be true until the contrary is proved.[112]

Presumptions *juris et de jure* hold a fact to be absolutely true

[98] Can. 1791, §2.
[99] Can. 1814.
[100] Cans. 1747, §2; 1904; 1972; 1015, §2; 1086, §1; 1814.
[101] Can. 1747, §1.
[102] Can. 1747, §3.
[103] Can. 1791.
[104] Can. 1751.
[105] Can. 1791, §1.
[106] Can. 1791, §2.
[107] Can. 1758.
[108] Can. 1817.
[109] Can. 1826.
[110] Can. 1825, §1.
[111] Can. 1825, §2.
[112] Can. 1826.

in such a manner as to not admit generally speaking of a proof to the contrary, or in other words the fact on which it is based must be overthrown to disprove it.[113]

Two canons in the Code establish a *presumptio juris et de jure,* viz., Canon 1904, a matter adjudged; and Canon 1972, concerning a marriage not disputed during life. Against a *presumptio juris et de jure,* proof must be given which will overthrow the fact upon which the presumption is based. For example, in the case of a *res judicata* of Canon 1904, while the justice of the sentence can never be attacked, one may prove that there is no basis for the suit. Presumptions *juris tantum* are to be found in several canons. A few directly pertaining to marriage are used here.

For example the presumption of law is always in favor of marriage until the contrary is proved by full canonical proof, excluding any reasonable doubt to the contrary, excepting the prescriptions of Canon 1127, where in doubtful cases law favors the privilege of faith. Hence, in all cases except where there is a question of the Pauline Privilege, a marriage positively doubtful and probably null is held to be valid in the external forum until the nullity is legitimately and certainly established.[114]

A doubt concerning a marriage may arise in two ways. It may first arise in regard to the validity of a marriage certainly performed, and secondly in regard to the actual celebration of the marriage.

It is clear that any doubt as to a certainly performed marriage is resolved in favor of the marriage. This is clearly the meaning of Canon 1014. A doubt in regard to the actual celebration of a marriage is not so clearly indicated in Canon 1014, but it is resolved in favor of the marriage according to the practice of the Holy Office.[115] In this case marriage is said to be in possession, since the parties are in good faith and consider themselves married, and as a result no scandal arises. A marriage entered into with a dispensation and a doubt arises as to whether the dispensation was valid, the presumption is in favor of the validity of the dispensation

[113] Can. 1826.

[114] Gasparri, *De Matrimonio,* I, 217.

[115] Cfr. Coll. S. C. de P. F., 2, 1465, 2°, 1392. Payen, *De Matrimonio* I, p. 86. sq.

and consequently of the marriage, until the contrary is proved.[116] This presumption favors not only the marriages of Catholics, but also the marriages of heretics and of infidels which have the appearance of a valid marriage, with the exception of the privilege of Canon 1127. Of course if the semblance or appearance of a true marriage is lacking the presumption is not in favor of such marriages.[117] When a person already married contracts a second marriage while his or her spouse is still alive, the validity is in favor of the first and not the second marriage. The burden of proof of the invalidity of the first marriage falls upon the person who wishes to marry again, or on the promoter of justice if the first marriage has been denounced to him.

The validity of a doubtfully valid second marriage contracted in good faith is to be upheld, if at the time of the second marriage one of the parties of the first marriage was held certainly to be dead, until it is established juridically that at the time of the second marriage, the party supposed to have been dead was alive.

Canon 1015, §2, presumes the consummation of marriage until the contrary is proved. Canon 1086, §1, presumes internal consent to be in conformity with the external manifestation against all of these direct and indirect proofs to the contrary is admissible.

In regard to presumptions, not stated in the Code, the legislator determines that they shall not be conjectured by a judge except from a certain specific fact which is directly connected with the fact in controversy.[118] A natural presumption (*ab homine*) must be a reasonable conclusion or inference from another specific fact already established by evidence in the case. These personal presumptions may be weak, strong or very strong. They create only a probability greater or lesser according to their circumstances, but not a complete proof.

Burden of Proof. The burden of proof in matrimonial causes always falls upon the plaintiff or person who attacks the validity of the marriage. It does not fall upon the defendant. This holds

[116] *A.A.S.*, II (1910), 585.

[117] Vermeersch-Creusen, *Epitome*, II, n. 227.

[118] Can. 1828.

whether the plaintiff is one of the parties or both, or the defender of the bond, or the promoter of justice. The burden of proof can fall on the defendant only when there is a presumption of law for the plaintiff, or when the defendant takes an exception by which he affirms something.

CHAPTER IX

THE SENTENCE

AFTER the advocates of both parties have finished their defense and the defender of the bond has declared that he has nothing further to say, the next step in the process of a matrimonial cause is the pronouncing of the sentence.

A sentence is either interlocutory or definitive. A sentence is interlocutory, if it decides an incidental question connected with the matrimonial cause. Interlocutory sentences may be given in the form of a decree, or in a formal judicial manner as described in a previous chapter.* The definitive sentence in a matrimonial cause is the act of the tribunal by which it defines and announces in the manner prescribed by law that the marriage in question is either valid or invalid.

At the close of the defense arguments, each judge shall be furnished with a complete copy of the records of the case.

After the judges have received a copy of the records of the case or the original acts, if copies have not been made, each judge shall study the record and prepare the written conclusion which he is obliged to submit according to Canon 1871, §1, at the meeting prescribed by the Code for defining the sentence. Great care should be taken against the loss or the misplacing of any of these documents. Judges should likewise avoid delay in preparing their opinions, not defer study of the case until there is insufficient time left for that careful and diligent study of the case which is required of the judge in formulating an opinion. He shall go over the evidence of both sides, weigh it impartially in the light of prescriptions of the Code relative to the cause in question. He should frame his opinion so as to include and settle all points of the controversy mentioned in the bill of complaint. He may pursue a course similar to that recommended to the advocate in preparing his defense, i. e., divide his opinion into various separate heads corresponding to the different points of the controversy and enumerate

* Cfr. p. 66.

the proofs supporting or militating against each point and then formulate his opinion. If the proving force of the evidence is given in the Code he must follow the legal rule. If the proving force of an argument is left to his own discretion he must follow his conscience, and sincerely and impartially decide to the best of his ability the value of the arguments presented in the acts and proofs, and decide whether these arguments are decisive or weak, keeping in mind the character of the witness. If the acts and proofs are such as to establish in his mind moral certitude against the validity of the marriage he should formulate his conclusion accordingly.[1] If he cannot arrive at moral certitude, if there exists in his mind a prudent doubt about the invalidity of the marriage, if the evidence for the invalidity is insufficient, he must pronounce in favor of the validity of the marriage, as the presumption is in favor of marriage, until the contrary is proved.[2] In his written opinion each judge must state the reasons in fact and in law which enabled him to arrive at the conclusions expressed in the opinion.[3] In other words, the main and substantial grounds for the opinion should be given in full, and should be taken from the canonical proofs submitted during the trial, not from any personal or extrajudicial information, but solely on the information and proofs adduced during the trial. The judge should, therefore, in his opinion review the evidence offered on both sides, clearly and fully though without any unnecessary length or superfluous detail and show how, according to the law of the Church, it proves or disproves the validity of the marriage in the case.

Art. I. The Meeting of the Judges

Preliminary Meeting. The recommendation of Noval[4] that a preliminary meeting be held some days before the final meeting in which the definitive sentence is drafted is very practical. At this preliminary meeting the *ponens* who by the fact of his appointment should devote special and diligent study to the case in which he is acting as *ponens,* may present the results of his study and observa-

[1] Can. 1869, §1, S2.
[2] Can. 1014.
[3] Can. 1871, §2.
[4] Noval, *De Processibus,* n. 137.

tion to the other judges. He may recall to them the various parts of evidence presented, and the different witnesses who testified, suggesting any inconsistencies or improbabilities he has observed. He may caution the judges about such evidence as is likely to appear entitled to too much or to too little weight, about evidence that is inherently weak or strong. In general he will undertake to present to the other judges a well balanced yet brief summary and analysis of the case. This summary will be of immense value to the other judges in aiding them to formulate the written opinion which each judge must bring to the final meeting in which the definitive sentence is drafted.

Final Meeting. On the day, and at the hour, and in the place appointed by the Official, the judges having previously been notified, shall assemble for deliberation on the definitive sentence. Each judge shall bring to this meeting his written conclusions on the case, together with a statement of the motives that prompt them. The three judges alone, to the exclusion of everyone else, are present at this meeting.[5]

The *ponens* in the case briefly explains the reasons why the case was introduced, what the plaintiff asks, and what the defendant admits or denies, what proofs were produced, what the conclusions of the litigants are, what incidental causes were proposed, and how they were settled, and what ones if any are left to be solved, and whatever processural defects that may exist. He will then propose the formula of doubt. *"An constet de matrimonii nullitate in casu,"* or *"an constet de matrimonii nullitate ex vi et metu,"* mentioning whatever the defect or impediment is, on which the petition for a declaration of nullity is based.

The *ponens* will then read his opinion in which he shall declare either in favor or against the nullity of the marriage.

After the *ponens,* the Official and the other synodal or associate judge read their opinions. All the judges must bring a written opinion and all *must* vote on the case.

A moderate discussion will follow in order to determine the wording of the decisive part of the sentence.

[5] Can. 1871, §2.

During this discussion any judge may change his opinion or vote, to agree with the opinion of his colleagues, either in part or in its entirety, by expressing in writing at the end of his opinion the changes induced and the reasons for them. This form may be used *"Accedo voto Domini . . . et ob rationes in eodem voto expressas"* or *"ob rationes . . . etc."* [6]

If the decision of the judges is unanimous, formulating the definitive sentence will present no difficulties. If the decision of the judges is not unanimous the opinion of the majority will become the opinion of the tribunal. If the judges cannot reach an agreement on the decision in the first discussion, and no judge sees fit to change his opinion, the decision may be reserved for another meeting which must be held not later than the eighth day after the first meeting.[7] If the delay in reaching a decision is due to lack of evidence on some point, or because some new and necessary question occurred, this certainly would constitute the grave cause required by Canon 1786 for requestioning witnesses or parties after the *conclusio in causa* in the hope that this new evidence might throw light on the controverted points. In event that no decision is reached at this final meeting recourse should be had to the Ordinary to substitute other judges.[8]

Art. II. Contents and Form of Sentence

The *ponens* [9] writes the definitive sentence. The majority of the judges may determine which motives, i.e., reasons of fact and of law, are to be advanced in the sentence, otherwise it is left to the discretion of the *ponens* to select from the motives given by the judges in their conclusions those which shall be contained in the sentence. The sentence must clearly and unequivocally decide for or against the invalidity of the marriage and offer suitable answers to each point obtained in the *libellus*. A conditional sentence

[6] Can. 1871, §4.

[7] Can. 1871, §5.

[8] Muniz, *o. c.*, III, p. 417, and Vidal (Wernz-Vidal), *o. c.*, VI, p. 545, would ask the Ordinary to add other judges, e.g., to add two more judges to the three already hearing the case.

[9] The *ponens* is called *extensor* in Canon 1873, §3.

or a sentence which would leave the matter in doubt would be invalid. It should likewise contain the amount of expenses incurred and state by whom they are to be paid.

A sentence begins with an invocation of the Divine Name, such as "*In nomine Domini Amen.*" Then follow the names of the three judges, beginning with the Official, the other coming in the order of precedence. Next come the names of the plaintiff and defendant (indicating their domiciles), and after each one the names of their procurators and advocates. Then follows the name of the defender of the bond and of the promoter of justice if he took part in the trial.

A brief history or statement of the case then follows, stating (a) the impediment as set forth and affirmed by the plaintiff and as denied by the defendant or the defender of the bond; (b) that both parties were present during the trial or that one of them was absent contumaciously; (c) that the main and substantial formalities of a trial as prescribed by law took place.

A statement of the motives of fact *(in facto)* is given, followed by a statement of the motives of law *(in jure)* on which the sentence is based, which means that the law is applied to the various points taken from the evidence advanced during the trial to show how it proves or disproves the invalidity of the marriage.

Then comes the dispositive or definitive part of the sentence, usually introduced by a phrase similar to this: "*Quibus omnibus, tum in jure tum in facto, perpensis, Nos infrascripti Judices, pro Tribunali sedentes, et solum Deum prae oculis habentes, Christi nomine invocato, decernimus, declaramus et definitive sententiamus.*" There follows then the answer to the formula of doubt—"*constare*" *or* "*non constare de nullitate matrimonii inter . . . actorem et . . . partem conventam.*" The expenses of the case and assessment of the expenses are then expressed. At the bottom of the sentence follows the day, month, year, and place, when and where the sentence was drafted, and the signatures of all the judges and the notary, and the seal of the tribunal. All judges—even the dissenting judge—must sign the sentence and no minority opinion is expressed in the sentence.[10]

[10] Roberti, *De Processibus II*, p. 118.

Art. III. Publication of the Sentence

As soon as possible after the sentence is drafted it should be published. Sentence may be published in three ways: (a) By summoning the parties to court to hear the sentence solemnly read in court; (b) by notifying the parties that a copy is ready at the Chancery and permission is granted to read it or to have a copy made; (c) by sending a copy of the sentence to the parties or their procurators through the mail, or through the courier of the tribunal. Registered mail should be used and the return receipt is to be filed with the acts of the case. If the sentence is delivered by a messenger of the tribunal, he should make a report to the tribunal in the same manner in which he reported the citations. A copy of the sentence should be sent to the defender of the bond, together with notification, if the sentence given was for the nullity of the marriage, that he should appeal within ten days. Notification should be sent to the plaintiff and the defendant telling them of their respective rights to appeal, and that the appeal should be taken within ten days, and reminding the plaintiff, if the sentence declared the marriage null, that the sentence cannot be executed until another conformable sentence for nullity is passed by a court of appeal.

The right of appeal from the tribunal of the court of first instance lies with the party against whom the first sentence was passed and with the defender of the bond. If the first sentence was for the validity of the marriage the defender does not appeal, although the party against whom the sentence was given may appeal. If the first sentence was for the nullity of the marriage the defender must appeal. If he neglects to fulfill his duty, he may be compelled to appeal by the tribunal.[11]

Notice of appeal must be brought before the tribunal which passed sentence within ten days from the time the party or defender received notification of the sentence. These ten days are computed according to Canon 34, §3, n. 3, hence the first day, that is, the day on which the notification was received, is not counted and one has ten full days after that day before the time will expire during

[11] Can. 1986.

which the notice of the appeal must be filed. Hence if notification of the sentence was received on the sixth of March—the time for filing an appeal expires at midnight of the sixteenth of March.

In a matrimonial cause two conformable sentences must have been given before the parties are free to enter another marriage. If the decision of the court of appeal confirms the sentence of the diocesan tribunal and the defender of the metropolitan curia does not in conscience consider that an appeal should be taken to the third instance, then the parties are free to marry ten days after the second conformable sentence has been given.[12] These ten days permit the defender to file notice of appeal before the tribunal which gave this second sentence.[13] Once the defender files notice of appeal the parties are not able to contract new marriages, for the appeal suspends the second sentence so the parties cannot act upon it.[14] As causes concerning the state of a person never become settled (*res iudicata*), no matter how many sentences have been given,[15] the sentence in a matrimonial cause is never absolutely final. There is always the possibility of the case being reopened if new arguments are found.[16] When the court of appeal informs the local curia that the first sentence of the invalidity of the bond has been upheld it becomes the duty of the Ordinary of the place where the first trial was held to have this declaration of nullity inscribed in the baptismal and matrimonial registers where the marriage had been recorded.[17]

[12] Can. 1987.
[13] Can. 1881.
[14] Can. 1889.
[15] Can. 1902.
[16] Cans. 1989, 1903.
[17] Can. 1988. Noval, *De Iudiciis,* n. 870.

BIBLIOGRAPHY

Sources

Acta Apostolicae Sedis (AAS), Romae, 1909—

Acta Sanctae Sedis (ASS), 41 vols., Romae, 1865-1908.

Canones et Decreta Concilii Tridentini, 19 ed., Taurini, 1913.

Codex Iuris Canonici Pii X Pontificis Maximi iussu digestu Benedicti Papae XV auctoritate promulgatus, Romae, 1918.

Codicis Iuris Canonici Fontes, 4 vols., Romae, 1923-1926.

Collectanea Sacrae Congregationis de Propaganda Fide (Coll.) 2 vols., Romae, 1907.

Collectio Lacensis, Acta et Decreta Sacrorum Conciliorum Recentiorum (Coll. Lacen.), 7 vols., Friburgi Br., 1870-1890.

Concilii Plenarii Baltimorensis II, Acta et Decreta, Baltimore, 1894.

Concilii Plenarii Baltimorensis III, Acta et Decreta, Baltimore, 1884.

Corpus Iuris Canonici, Editio Lipsiensis II., 2 vols., Lipsiae, 1922.

Corpus Iuris Civilis, Berolini, 3 vols., 1928-1929.

Denzinger-Bannwart, *Enchiridion Symbolorum Definitionum et Declarationum de Rebus Fidei et Morum,* 14-15 ed., Friburgi B., 1922.

Mansi, Joannes, *Sacrorum Conciliorum Nova et Amplissima Collectio,* 53 vols., Paris, 1901-1927.

Regulae Servandae in Iudiciis apud S Romanae Rotae Tribunal, Romae, 1910.

Regulae Servandae in Iudiciis apud Supremum Signaturae Apostolicae Tribunal, Romae, 1912.

Regulae Servandae in Processibus super Matrimonio Rato et Non Consummato, etc., Romae, 1923.

Thesaurus Resolutionum Sacrae Congregationis Concilii, 167 vols., Romae, 1718-1908.

Works of Reference

Aertnys-Damen, *Theologia Moralis,* 11 ed., 2 vols., Taurini, 1928.

Aichner, *Compendium Iuris Ecclesiastici,* 9 ed., Brixinae, 1900.

Augustine, *A Commentary on Canon Law,* 3 ed., 7 vols., St. Louis, 1923.

Ayrinhac, *Marriage Legislation in the New Code of Canon Law,* New York, 1918.

Badii, *Institutiones Iuris Canonici,* 2 vols., Florentiae, 1921.

Barbosa, *Jus Pontificium Universum,* Lugduni, 1556.

Bargilliat, *Praelectiones Iuris Canonici,* 2 vols., Paris, 1915.

Bassibey, *Le Mariage devant les Tribunaux Ecclesiastiques,* Paris, 1899.

Benedict XIV, *Opera Omnia,* 17 vols., Prati, 1839-1847.

Benedict XIV, *De Synodo Diocesana,* 2 ed., 2 vols., Parmae, 1764.
Bernardus Papiensis, *Summa Decretalium,* ed Laspreyres, Ratisbon, 1840.
Blat, *Commentarium Textus Codicis Iuris Canonici,* Liber IV, *De Processibus,* Romae, 1927.
Bouix, *De Iudiciis Ecclesiasticis,* 3 ed., 2 vols., Paris, 1883.
Bouuaert-Simenon, *Manuale Iuris Canonici,* 2 ed., Gandae et Leodii, 1926.
Cappello, *De Curia Romana,* Romae, 1911.
Cappello, *Tractatus Canonico-Moralis de Sacramentis,* Taurini, 3 vols., 1923: vol. III (1927).
Cerato, *Matrimonium a Codice I.C. integre desumptum,* 4 ed., Patavii, 1927.
Cerchiari, E., *Sancta Romana Rota,* 4 vols., Romae, 1921.
Chelodi, *Ius Matrimoniale,* 3 ed., Tridenti, 1921.
Chelodi, *Ius de Personis,* Tridenti, 1925.
Cicognani, *Commentarium ad Librum I Codicis,* Romae, 1925.
Cicognani, *Ius Canonicum,* Romae, 1925.
Cimetier, *Pour Etudier le Code de Droit Canonique,* Paris, 1927.
Cocchi, *Commentarium in Codicem Iuris Canonici,* 7 vols., Turin, 1925-1927.
Coronata, *Institutiones Juris Canonici,* Taurini, 1924.
D'Angelo, S., *La Curia Diocesana,* 4 vols. (1928), Giarre (Sicilia).
De Angelis, *Praelectiones Iuris Canonici,* 5 vols., Romae, 1908.
De Becker, *De Sponsalibus et Matrimonio,* Bruxellis, 1896.
De Lugo, Joannes, *Disputationes Scholasticae et Morales,* 8 vols., Paris, 1868-1869.
De Smet, *De Sponsalibus et Matrimonio,* 4 ed., Brugis, 1927.
De Smet, *Praxis Matrimonialis,* 3 ed., Brugis, 1920.
Devoti, *Institutiones Canonicae,* Leodii, 1883.
Devoti, *Ius Canonicum Universum Publicum et Privatum,* 3 vols., Romae, 1837.
Droste-Messmer, *Canonical Procedure in Disciplinary and Criminal Cases of Clerics,* New York, 1887.
Dugan, *The Judiciary Department of the Diocesan Curia,* Washington, 1925.
Engelmann-Millar, *History of Continental Legal Procedure,* vol. VII, Continental Legal History Series, Boston, 1927.
Esmein, *Le Mariage en Droit Canonique,* 2 vols., Paris, 1891.
Farrugia, *De Matrimonio et Causis Matrimonialibus,* Taurini, 1924.
Ferraris, *Prompta Bibliotheca Canonica,* 9 vols., Romae, 1885-1892.
Ferreres, *Institutiones Canonici,* Ed. II, Barcinone, 1920.
Fournier, Edouard, *Les origines du Vicaire General,* Paris, 1922.
——— *Le Vicaire General ou moyen age.*
Funk, *Didascalia et Constitutiones Apostolorum,* Paderbornae, 1905.
Gasparri, *Tractatus Canonicus de Matrimonio,* 3 ed., 2 vols., Paris, 1904.
Hefele, *Conciliengeschichte,* 2 ed., 9 vols., Freiburg Br., 1873-1890.
Hefele-Clarke, *A History of the Christian Councils,* Transl., 2 vols., Edinburgh, 1876-1883.
Heiner, *Der Kirchliche Strafprozess,* Koln, 1910.

Heiner-Wynen, *De Processu Criminali Ecclesiastico,* Romae, 1912.
Hurter, *Theologiae Dogmaticae Compendium,* 6 ed., 3 vols., Oeniponte, 1889.
Hilling, Nikolaus, *Das Eherecht des Codex Juris Canonici,* Freiburg in Br., 1927.
Lanier, *Guide Practique de Procedure Matrimoniale,* Paris, 1927.
Lega, *Praelectiones in Textum Iuris Canonici de Iudiciis Ecclesiasticis,* 2 vols., Romae, 1898.
Leitner, *Handbuch des Katholischen Kirchenrechts,* ed. II, Regensburg, 1918.
Lightfoot, *The Apostolic Fathers,* London, 1893.
Mansella, *De Impedimentis Matrimonium Dirimentibus ac de Processu Iudiciali,* Romae, 1881.
Maroto, *Institutiones Iuris Canonici,* 2 vols., Romae, 1919-1921.
Migne, *Encyclopedie Theologique,* 50 vols., Paris, 1846.
Migne, *Patrologia Graeca,* 161 vols., Paris, 1858-1864.
Migne, *Patrologia Latina,* 221 vols., Paris, 1847-1870.
Molitor, W., *Ueber Kanonisches Gerichtsverfaharen gegen Cleriker,* Mainz, 1856.
Monin, *De Curia Romana,* Louvain, 1912.
Muniz, T., *Procedimientos Ecclesiasticos,* 3 vols., Levilla.
Noval, *Commentarium Codicis Iuris Canonici,* Liber IV. *De Processibus,* Pars I De Iudiciis, Romae, 1920.
Oesterle, *Praelectiones Juris Canonici,* Tom. I, Romae, 1931.
Oietti, B., *Commentarium in Codicem,* 3 vols., Romae, 1927.
Pallavicini, *Istoria del Concilio di Trento,* 4 vols., Romae, 1883.
Payen, *De Matrimonio,* 3 vols., China, 1928.
Peries, *Code de Procedure dans les Causes Matrimoniales,* Paris, 1894.
Perrone, *De Matrimonio Christiano Libri Tres.,* 3 vols., Leodii, 1861.
Pertile, *Storia della procedura,* ed. II, 4 vols., Torino, 1896-1902.
Pighi, *De Sacramento Matrimonii,* Veronae, 1919.
Pirhing, *Jus Canonicum in Quinque Libros Decretalium Distributum Venetiis,* 1759.
Prummer, Dominicus, *Manuale Iuris Canonici,* 3 ed., Friburgi Brisgoviae, 1922.
Reiffenstuel, *Jus Canonicum Universum,* 4 vols., Venetiis, 1735.
Roberti, *De Processibus,* vol. I, Romae, 1926.
Roskovany, *Matrimonium in Ecclesia Catholica Potestati Ecclesiasticae Subjectum: cum amplissima collectione monumentorum et literatura,* 4 vols., Pestini-Nitriae, 1870-1882.
Richter, *Canones et Decreta Concilii Tridentini,* Lipsiae, 1853.
Santi-Leitner, *Praelectiones Iuris Canonici,* 4 vols., Ratisbonnae, 1899.
Schalz, Carolus, *De Instituto Officialis sive Vicarii Generalis Episcopi,* Vratislaviae, 1899.
Schmalzgrueber, Franciscus, *Jus Ecclesiasticum Universum,* 12 vols., Romae, 1843-1845.
Smith, *The Marriage Process in the United States,* New York, 1893.
Thomassinus, *Vetus et Nova Ecclesiae Disciplina,* Mogontiaci, 1787.
Toso, Al., *Commentaria Minora ad C.J.C.,* lib. II, P. I, Romae, 1921.

Van Howe, *Prolegomena*, 1929. *De Legibus Ecclesiasticis*, Romae, 1930.

Vermeersch-Creusen, *Epitome Iuris Canonici*, 3 ed., 3 vols., Mechliniae-Romae, I, II (1927), III (1928).

Vlaming, *Praelectiones Iuris Matrimonii*, 3 ed., 2 vols., Bussum, 1921.

Von Kienitz, *Generalvikar und Offizial*, Freiburg, 1931.

Vromant, *Jus Missionarium, De Personis*, Louvain, 1929.

Wernz, *Ius Decretalium*, 6 vols., Prati, 1911.

Wernz-Vidal, *Ius Canonicum*, 3 vols., Romae, 1923-1927.

Willoughby, *Principles of Judicial Administration*, Washington, 1929.

Woywod, Stanislaus, *A Practical Commentary on the Code of Canon Law*, 2 vols., New York, 1925.

Zitelli, *Apparatus Iuris Ecclesiastici*, 3 ed., Romae, 1903.

Periodicals

American Ecclesiastical Review (AER), Philadelphia, 1889—

Analecta Iuris Pontificii, Roma, 1855-1890.

Apollinaris, Roma, 1928—

Archiv fur katholisches Kirchenrecht (AfkK), Mains, 1885.

Ephemerides Theologicae Lovaniensis (ETL), Louvain-Brugis, 1924—

Homiletic and Pastoral Review, New York, 1900—

Ius Pontificium, Romae, 1921—

Nouvelle Revue Theologique (NRT), Paris, 1869—

Periodica, de Re Canonica et Morali, Romae et Brugis, 1905—

UNIVERSITAS CATHOLICA AMERICAE

WASHINGTON, D. C.

FACULTAS IURIS CANONICI

1931-1932

No. 78

DEUS LUX MEA

TITULI

QUOS

AD DOCTORATUS GRADUM

IN

JURE CANONICO

APUD UNIVERSITATEM CATHOLICAM AMERICAE

CONSEQUENDUM

PUBLICE PROPUGNABIT

AVITUS EDUARDUS LYONS

SACERDOS DIOCESIS TOLETANUS

LICENTIATUS IN JURE CANONICO

HORA IX DIE XXI MAII, A. D. MCMXXXII

TITULI

DE IURE CANONICO

I.	De Dissertatione.	
II.	Canones 1-7	De Ambitu Codicis.
III.	Canones 8-24	De Legibus Ecclesiasticis.
IV.	Canones 25-30	De Consuetudine.
V.	Canones 31-35	De Temporis Supputatione.
VI.	Canones 36-62	De Rescriptis.
VII.	Canones 63-79	De Privilegiis.
VIII.	Canones 80-86	De Dispensationibus.
IX.	Canones 87-107	Generales Notiones de Personis.
X.	Canones 111-117	De Clericorum Adscriptione Alicui Dioecesi.
XI.	Canones 118-123	De Juribus et Privilegiis Clericorum.
XII.	Canones 124-144	De Obligationibus Clericorum.
XIII.	Canones 145-195	De Officiis Ecclesiasticis.
XIV.	Canones 196-210	De Potestate Ordinaria et Delegata.
XV.	Canones 211-214	De Reductione Clericorum ad Statum Laicalem.
XVI.	Canones 487-498	De Notione Religionis, et de Erectione et Suppressione Religionis, Provinciae et Domus.
XVII.	Canones 538-586	De Admissione in Religionem.
XVIII.	Canones 592-631	De Obligationibus et Privilegiis Religiosorum.
XIX.	Canones 820-823	De Tempore et Loco Missae Celebrandae.
XX.	Canones 824-844	De Missarum Eleemosynis seu Stipendiis.
XXI.	Canones 1012-1018	De Matrimonio in Genere.
XXII.	Canones 1019-1034	De iis Matrimonii Celebrationi Praemitti Debent.
XXIII.	Canones 1035-1057	De Impedimentis in Genere.
XXIV.	Canones 1058-1066	De Impedimentis Impedientibus.
XXV.	Canones 1067-1080	De Impedimentis Dirimentibus.
XXVI.	Canones 1081-1093	De Consensu Matrimoniali.
XXVII.	Canones 1094-1103	De Forma Celebrationis Matrimonii.
XXVIII.	Canones 1110-1117	De Matrimonii Effectibus.
XXIX.	Canones 1552-1568	De Notione Iudicii et de Foro Competenti.
XXX.	Canones 1569-1607	De Variis Tribunalium Gradibus et Speciebus.
XXXI.	Canones 1608-1645	De Disciplina in Tribunalibus Servanda.
XXXII.	Canones 1646-1666	De Partibus in Causa.
XXXIII.	Canones 1667-1705	De Actionibus et Exceptionibus.
XXXIV.	Canones 1706-1725	De Causae Introductione.

XXXV.	Canones 1726-1746	De Litis Contestatione, de Litis Instantia, et de Interrogationibus Partibus in Judicio Faciendis.
XXVI.	Canones 1747-1836	De Probationibus.
XXXVII.	Canones 1837-1857	De Causis Incidentibus.
XXXVIII.	Canones 1858-1877	De Processus Publicatione, de Conclusione in Causa, de Causae Discussione, et de Sententia.
XXXIX.	Canones 2195-2198	De Natura Delicti Eiusque Divisione.
XL.	Canones 2199-2211	De Imputabilitate Delicti, de Causis Illam Aggravantibus vel Minuentibus et de Iuridicis Delicti Effectibus.
XLI.	Canones 2212-2213	De Conatu Delicti.
XLII.	Canones 2214-2240	De Poenis in Genere.
XLIII.	Canones 2241-2285	De Poenis Medicinalibus seu de Censuris.
XLIV.	Canones 2286-2305	De Poenis Vindicativis.
XLV.	Canones 2306-2313	De Remediis Poenalibus et Poenitentiis.

DE JURE ROMANO

XLVI. Historical Periods of Roman Law.
XLVII. The Sources of Roman Law.
XLVIII. Personality.
XLIX. Slavery.
L. Citizenship.
LI. Patria Potestas.
LII. Personae in Manu.
LIII. Personae in Mancipio.
LIV. Tutela et Cura.
LV. Ownership.
LVI. De Obligationibus in Genere.
LVII. De Obligationibus Extra-Contractualibus.
LVIII. Furtum.
LIX. Damnum Injuria Datum.
LX. Injuria.

AMERICAN CIVIL—CHURCH LAW

LXI. Juridical Status of the Church in the United States.
LXII. Methods of Holding Church Property.
LXIII. Tax Exemption.
LXIV. Marriage.
LXV. Cemeteries.

Vidit Facultas:
VALENTINUS T. SCHAAF, O.F.M., J.C.D., Vice-Decanus.
LUDOVICUS H. MOTRY, S.T.D., J.C.D., a Secretis.
FRANCISCUS J. LARDONE, S.T.D., J.U.D.
JOHN McDILL FOX, A.B., LL.B.
Vidit Rector Magnificus Universitatis:
JACOBUS HUGO RYAN, S.T.D., PH.D., LL.D., LITT.D.

BIOGRAPHICAL NOTE

Avitus E. Lyons was born June 17, 1898, at Lima, Ohio. He received his elementary education at St. Rose Parish School, and his secondary training in St. Rose High School of that city. He pursued the prescribed courses of philosophy and theology in Mt. St. Mary's Seminary of the West, Cincinnati, Ohio, and was ordained priest July 16, 1922. The following nine years were spent in the service of the Diocese of Toledo. In the fall of 1931 he entered the Catholic University to pursue a graduate course of studies in Canon Law.

CANON LAW STUDIES

1. Freriks, Rev. Celestine A., C.PP.S., J.C.D., Religious Congregations in Their External Relations, 121 pp., 1916.
2. Galliher, Rev. Daniel M., O.P., J.C.D., Canonical Elections, 117 pp., 1917.
3. Borkowski, Rev. Aurelius L., O.F.M., De Confraternitatibus Ecclesiasticis, 136 pp., 1918.
4. Castillo, Rev. Cayo, J.C.D., Disertacion Historico-canonica sobre la Potestad del Cabildo en Sede Vacante o Impedida del Vicario Capitular, 99 pp., 1919 (1918).
5. Kubelbeck, Rev. William J., S.T.B., J.C.D., The Sacred Penitentiaria and Its Relations to Faculties of Ordinaries and Priests, 129 pp., 1918.
6. Petrovits, Rev. Joseph J. C., S.T.D., J.C.D., The New Church Law on Matrimony, X-461 pp., 1919.
7. Hickey, Rev. John J., S.T.B., J.C.D., Irregularities and Simple Impediments in the New Code of Canon Law, 100 pp., 1920.
8. Klekotka, Rev. Peter J., S.T.B., J.C.D., Diocesan Consultors, 179 pp., 1920.
9. Wannenmacher, Rev. Francis, J.C.D., The Evidence in Ecclesiastical Procedure Affecting the Marriage Bond, 1920. (Not Printed.)
10. Golden, Rev. Henry Francis, J.C.D., Parochial Benefices in the New Code, IV-119 pp., 1921. (Printed 1925.)
11. Koudelka, Rev. Charles J., J.C.D., Pastors, Their Rights and Duties According to the New Code of Canon Law, 211 pp., 1921.
12. Melo, Rev. Antonius, O.F.M., J.C.D., De Exemptione Regularium, X-188 pp., 1921.
13. Schaaf, Rev. Valentine Theodore, O.F.M., S.T.B., J.C.D., The Cloister, X-180 pp., 1921.
14. Burke, Rev. Thomas Joseph, S.T.B., J.C.D., Competence in Ecclesiastical Tribunals, IV-117 pp., 1922.
15. Leech, Rev. George Leo, J.C.D., A Comparative Study of the Constitution "Apostolicae Sedis" and the "Codex Juris Canonici," 179 pp., 1922.
16. Motry, Rev. Hubert Louis, S.T.D., J.C.D., Diocesan Faculties according to the Code of Canon Law, II-167 pp., 1922.
17. Murphy, Rev. George Lawrence, J.C.D., Delinquencies and Penalties in the Administration and the Reception of the Sacraments, IV-121 pp., 1923.
18. O'Reilly, Rev. John Anthony, S.T.B., J.C.D., Ecclesiastical Sepulture in the New Code of Canon Law, II-129 pp., 1923.
19. Michalicka, Rev. Wenceslas Cyrill, O.S.B., J.C.D., Judicial Procedure in Dismissal of Clerical Exempt Religious, 107 pp., 1923.
20. Dargin, Rev. Edward Vincent, S.T.B., J.C.D., Reserved Cases According to the Code of Canon Law, IV-103 pp., 1924.
21. Godfrey, Rev. John A., S.T.B., J.C.D., The Right of Patronage According to the Code of Canon Law, 153 pp., 1924.
22. Hagedorn, Rev. Francis Edward, J.C.D., General Legislation on Indulgences, II-154 pp., 1924.

23. King, Rev. James Ignatius, J.C.D., The Administration of the Sacraments to Dying Non-Catholics, V-141 pp., 1924.
24. Winslow, Rev. Francis Joseph, A.F.M., J.C.D., Vicars and Prefects Apostolic, IV-149 pp., 1924.
25. Correa, Rev. Jose Servelion, S.T.L., J.C.D., La Potestad Legislativa de la Iglesia Católica, IV-127 pp., 1925.
26. Dugan, Rev. Henry Francis, M.A., J.C.D., The Judiciary Department of the Diocesan Curia, 87 pp., 1925.
27. Keller, Rev. Charles Frederick, S.T.B., J.C.D., Mass Stipends, 167 pp., 1925.
28. Paschang, Rev. John Linus, J.C.D., The Sacramentals According to the Code of Canon Law, 129 pp., 1925.
29. Piontek, Rev. Cyrillus, O.F.M., S.T.B., J.C.D., De Indulto Exclaustrationis necnon Saecularizationis, XIII-289 pp., 1925.
30. Kearney, Rev. Richard Joseph, S.T.B., J.C.D., Sponsors at Baptism According to the Code of Canon Law, IV-127 pp., 1925.
31. Bartlett, Rev. Chester Joseph, A.M., LL.B., J.C.D., The Tenure of Parochial Property in the United States of America, V-108 pp., 1926.
32. Kilker, Rev. Adrian Jerome, J.C.D., Extreme Unction, V-425 pp., 1926.
33. McCormick, Rev. Robert Emmett, J.C.D., Confessors of Religious, VIII-266 pp., 1926.
34. Miller, Rev. Newton Thomas, J.C.D., Founded Masses According to the Code of Canon Law, VII-93 pp., 1926.
35. Roelker, Rev. Edward G., S.T.D., J.C.D., Principles of Privilege According to the Code of Canon Law, XI-166 pp., 1926.
36. Bakalarczyk, Rev. Richardus, M.I.C., J.U.D., De Novitiatu, VIII-208 pp., 1927.
37. Pizzuti, Rev. Lawrence, O.F.M., J.U.L., De Parochis Religiosis, 1927. (Not Printed.)
38. Bliley, Rev. Nicholas Martin, O.S.B., J.C.D., Altars According to the Code of Canon Law, XIX-132 pp., 1927.
39. Brown, Brendan Francis, A.B., LL.M., J.U.D., The Canonical Juristic Personality with Special Reference to its Status in the United States of America, V-212 pp., 1927.
40. Cavanaugh, Rev. William Thomas. C.P., J.U.D., The Reservation of the Blessed Sacrament, VIII-101 pp., 1927.
41. Doheny, Rev. William J., C.S.C., A.B., J.U.D., Church Property: Modes of Acquisition, X-118 pp., 1927.
42. Feldhaus, Rev. Aloysius H., C.PP.S., J.C.D., Oratories, IX-141 pp., 1927.
43. Kelly, Rev. James Patrick, A.B., J.C.D., The Jurisdiction of the Simple Confessor, X-208 pp., 1927.
44. Neuberger, Rev. Nicholas J., J.C.D., Canon 6 or the Relation of the Codex Juris Canonici to the Preceding Legislation, V-95 pp., 1927.
45. O'Keeffe, Rev. Gerald Michael, J.C.D., Matrimonial Dispensations, Powers of Bishops, Priests, and Confessors, VIII-232 pp., 1927.
46. Quigley, Rev. Joseph, A.M., A.B., J.C.D., Condemned Societies, 139 pp., 1927.
47. Zaplotnik, Rev. Ioannes Leo, J.C.D., De Vicariis Foraneis, X-142 pp., 1927.

48. Duskie, Rev. John Aloysius, A.B., J.C.D., The Canonical Status of the Orientals in the United States, VIII-196 pp., 1928.
49. Hyland, Rev. Francis Edward, J.C.D., Excommunication, Its Nature, Historical Development and Effects, VIII-181 pp., 1928.
50. Reinmann, Rev. Gerald Joseph, O.M.C., J.C.D., The Third Order Secular of Saint Francis, 201 pp., 1928.
51. Schenk, Rev. Francis J., J.C.D., The Matrimonial Impediments of Mixed Religion and Disparity of Cult, XVI-318 pp., 1929.
52. Coady, Rev. John Joseph, S.T.D., J.U.D., A.M., The Appointment of Pastors, VIII-150 pp., 1929.
53. Kay, Rev. Thomas Henry, J.C.D., Competence in Matrimonial Procedure, VIII-164 pp., 1929.
54. Turner, Rev. Sidney Joseph, C.P., J.U.D., The Vow of Poverty, XLIX-217 pp., 1929.
55. Kearney, Rev. Raymond A., A.B., S.T.D., J.C.D., The Principles of Delegation, VII-149 pp., 1929.
56. Conran, Rev. Edward James, A.B., J.C.D., The Interdict, V-163 pp., 1930.
57. O'Neil, Rev. William H., J.C.D., Papal Rescripts of Favor, VII-218 pp.,
58. Bastnagel, Rev. Clement Vincent, J.U.D., The Appointment of Parochial Adjutants and Assistants, XV-257 pp., 1930.
59. Ferry, Rev. William A., A.B., J.C.D., Stole Fees, X-107 pp., 1930.
60. Costello, Rev. John Michael, A.B., J.C.D., Domicile and Quasi-Domicile, VII-201 pp., 1930.
61. Kremer, Rev. Michael Nicholas, A.B., S.T.B., J.C.D., Church Support in the United States, VI-136 pp., 1930.
62. Angulo, Rev. Luis, C.M., J.C.D., Legislación de la Iglesia sobre la intención en la aplicación de la Santa Misa, VII-104 pp., 1931.
63. Frey, Rev. Wolfgang Norbert, O.S.B., A.B., J.C.D., The Act of Religious Profession, VIII-174 pp., 1931.
64. Roberts, Rev. James Brendan, A.B., J.C.D., The Banns of Marriage, XIV-140 pp., 1931.
65. Ryder, Rev. Raymond Aloysius, A.B., J.C.D., Simony, IX-151 pp., 1931.
66. Campagna, Rev. Angelo, Ph.D., J.U.D., Il Vicario Generale del Vescovo, VII-205 pp., 1931.
67. Cox, Rev. Joseph Godfrey, A.B., J.C.D., The Administration of Seminaries, VI-124 pp., 1931.
68. Gregory, Rev. Donald J., J.U.D., The Pauline Privilege, XV-165 pp., 1931.
60. Donohue, Rev. John F., J.C.D., The Impediment of Crime, VIII-110 pp., 1931.
70. Dooley, Rev. Eugene A., O.M.I., J.C.D., Church Law on Sacred Relics, IX-143 pp., 1931.
71. Orth, Rev. Clement Raymond, O.M.C., J.C.D., The Approbation of Religious Institutes, 171 pp., 1931.
72. Pernicone, Rev. Joseph M., A.B., J.C.D., The Ecclesiastical Prohibition of Books, XII-267 pp., 1932.
73. Clinton, Rev. Connell, A.B., J.C.L., The Paschal Precept, 1932.
74. Donnelly, Rev. Francis B., A.M., S.T.L., J.C.L., The Diocesan Synod, 1932

75. Torrente, Rev. Camilo, C.M.F., J.C.L., Las Processiones Sagradas, 1932.
76. Murphy, Rev. Edwin J., C.PP.S., J.C.L., Suspension Ex Informata Conscientia, 1932.
77. MacKenzie, Rev. Eric F., A.M., S.T.L., J.C.L., The Delict of Heresy in its Commission, Penalization, Absolution, 1932.
78. Lyons, Rev. Avitus E., S.T.B., J.C.L., The Collegiate Tribunal of First Instance, 1932.
79. Connolly, Rev. Thomas A., J.C.L., Appeals, 1932.
80. Sangmeister, Rev. Joseph V., A.B., J.C.L., Force and Fear as Precluding Matrimonial Consent, 1932.
81. Jaeger, Rev. Leo A., A.B., J.C.L., The Administration of Vacant and Quasi-Vacant Episcopal Sees in the United States, 1932.
82. Rimlinger, Rev. Herbert T., J.C.L., Error Invalidating Matrimonial Consent, 1932.
83. Barrett, Rev. John D. M., S.S., J.C.L., Comparative Study of the Third Plenary Council and the Code, 1932.

www.ingramcontent.com/pod-product-compliance
Lightning Source LLC
La Vergne TN
LVHW050227080826
844660LV00012B/484
* 9 7 8 0 8 1 3 2 2 2 6 7 7 *